PENGUIN BOOKS

SCIENCE OF EDUCATION AND THE PSYCHOLOGY OF THE CHILD

Jean Piaget was born in Neuchâtel, Switzerland. A child prodigy who originally became a biologist, he left biology with the desire to discover a sort of "embryology of intelligence." His world-renowned fame is primarily due to his comprehensive research in children's thought patterns and his general theory of intellectual development. M. Piaget is also the author of *Origins of Intelligence in Children, The Construction of Reality in the Child, Psychology and Epistemology, The Child and Reality, To Understand Is to Invent,* and numerous other books and articles. He is currently the director of the Rousseau Institute in Geneva.

*Science of Education and
the Psychology of the Child*

JEAN PIAGET

Translated from the French by Derek Coltman

PENGUIN BOOKS

Penguin Books Ltd, Harmondsworth,
Middlesex, England
Penguin Books, 625 Madison Avenue,
New York, New York 10022, U.S.A.
Penguin Books Australia Ltd, Ringwood,
Victoria, Australia
Penguin Books Canada Ltd, 41 Steelcase Road West,
Markham, Ontario, Canada
Penguin Books (N.Z.) Ltd, 182–190 Wairau Road,
Auckland 10, New Zealand

First published by Grossman Publishers,
a division of The Viking Press 1970
Viking Compass Edition published 1971
Reprinted 1971 (twice), 1972, 1974, 1975
Published in Penguin Books 1977
Psychologie et Pédagogie

LIBRARY OF CONGRESS CATALOGING IN PUBLICATION DATA

Piaget, Jean, 1896–
Science of education and the psychology of the child.

Translation of Psychologie et pédagogie.
Reprint of the 1971 ed. published by Grossman, New York.
Includes index.
1. Education—Addresses, essays, lectures.
2. Educational psychology—Addresses, essays, lectures.
I. Title.
[LB775.P48713 1976]   370.15   76-26177
ISBN 0 14 00.4377 2 (pbk.)

Printed in the United States of America by
Offset Paperback Mfrs., Inc., Dallas, Pennsylvania
Set in Linotype Times Roman

Contents

32192

Publishers' Foreword

The first of these texts dates from 1935, and forms the second part of our present publication. Focusing on the discoveries of genetic psychology, still not widely known at that time, it indicates their importance in the field of pedagogy and establishes their connection with the "active" educational methods that were then the subject of so much discussion.

The second text dates from 1965. We place it first in the present volume because it goes so far beyond the problems broached in the 1935 text as to be a discussion and a total reevaluation of our present pedagogy from the double point of view of methods and programs. It poses a problem of civilization.

It seemed to us important to make these two contributions from Jean Piaget available to the general public, because they are a great scientist's answer, based on a solid experimental foundation, to the present crisis, now a universal one, in education.

Part I *Education and Teaching since 1935*

Faced with so bold a task as attempting to sum up the development of education and teaching during the past thirty years, and the even bolder one of attempting to evaluate it, one is immediately seized by a genuine alarm at the disproportion that still subsists today, undiminished since 1935, between the immensity of the efforts that have been made and the absence of any fundamental renewal in our methods, in our programs, in the very position of our problems, or, indeed, in pedagogy as a whole considered as a guiding discipline.

In 1939, Lucien Febvre spoke of the violent and even brutal shock one experiences when one compares the empiricism of pedagogy with the "healthy, straightforward, and productive realism" of the psychological and sociological studies from which pedagogy might be expected to draw inspiration; and he explained this lag, or rather this lack of coordination, as resulting from the infinite complexity of our social life, of which education is at once the reflection and the instrument. This is no doubt true, but we are still left with the problem—one that becomes daily more worrying—of understanding how it is that we possess a science of medicine—even though its precepts achieve relatively little application in many countries and social strata—whereby governmental ministers of education, unlike those concerned with public health, are unable to rely upon an impartial and objective discipline with the authority to supply both principles and factual data, thus leaving only those problems concerned with determining the best applications. In short, ministers of health do not legislate in the sphere of medical knowledge because there already exists a science of medicine whose researches are both autonomous and generally encouraged by the state, whereas public educators are civil servants answerable to a ministry that decides not only upon applications but also upon the principles to be applied, simply because it lacks the support of a science of education sufficiently developed to be able to answer the innumerable questions that present themselves every day and whose solution is therefore left either to empiricism or to tradition.

To retrace the development of education and teaching from 1935 to the present day therefore involves taking stock of the immense quantitative progress in public schooling, noting a certain number of localized qualitative improvements, in particular where they have been encouraged by the many political and social changes in those years, but above all—since to ignore these preliminary considerations would falsify the entire picture—it means asking ourselves why the science of education has made so few advances compared with the profound new developments in child psychology and sociology itself.

1. Developments in Pedagogy

There can be no question here of taking theoretical considerations as our starting point. The only way to begin is with the facts that sooner or later make such considerations necessary. Three sorts of data, at once disparate and selected from among many others, are instructive in this respect.

Ignorance of Results

The first observation—a surprising one—that comes to mind after the passage of thirty years is the ignorance in which we still remain with regard to the results achieved by our educational techniques. In 1965 we do not know, any more than we did in 1935, what remains of the various kinds of knowledge acquired in primary and secondary schools, after five, ten, or twenty years, among representatives of the various strata of our population. Though we do, of course, possess indirect forms of information on this point, such as that provided by the post-school examinations given to conscripts into the Swiss army, the amazing story of which between the years 1875 and 1914 has been recorded for us by P. Bovet (and in particular the intensive revision courses organized in many localities in order to conceal the disastrous results these examinations produced when not prepared for by last-minute cramming). But we have no exact information, for example, as to what a thirty-year-old peasant still remembers of the history and geography he

was once taught, or as to how much a practicing lawyer may have
retained of the chemistry, physics, or even geometry he acquired in
his high school or lycée. We are told that Latin (and in certain
countries Greek as well) is indispensable to the training of a doctor
of medicine; but has anyone ever attempted to provide controls for
such an affirmation, and to dissociate it from the factors of interested professional protection involved, by trying to evaluate what
remains of such training in the mind of a practicing doctor (and
also by drawing the relevant comparison between Japanese and
Chinese doctors and European ones with regard to this relationship
between medical value and classical studies)? And yet the economists who collaborated on the General Plan for the French State
specifically asked that methods of checking our educational productivity be devised and put into practice.

It will be objected that our memory of what we have learned is
unrelated to the culture acquired; but how is one to evaluate that
culture other than by resorting to wildly generalized and subjective
judgments? And is the culture that counts in any particular individual always that which results from the specifically scholastic part of
his education (once the detailed knowledge acquired at final examination level has been forgotten), or is it the culture his school
managed to develop in him through incentives or interests stimulated independently of what at that time appeared to be the essential part of his so-called basic education? Even the central question
of the value of teaching dead languages, on the grounds that they
provide an exercise capable of transmitting beneficial effects to
other spheres of activity, remains as far from being decisively set-
tled by experiment today as it was thirty years ago, despite a certain number of British studies; so that the educator faced with having to give advice on such capital issues is reduced to relying not on
a body of knowledge but on considerations of good sense or mere
expediency (such as the number of careers inaccessible to any student who has not passed through the prescribed educational channel or stream).

Moreover, there are certain branches of instruction, quite obviously devoid of any formative value, that we continue to lay down

as essential without knowing whether in fact they do or do not attain the utilitarian end that has been traditionally allotted to them. Everyone accepts, for example, the fact that in order to live a social existence it is necessary to know how to spell (leaving aside any discussion of the rational or purely traditionalist significance of such a necessity). But we continue to lack all decisive knowledge of whether specialized instruction in orthography increases our learning ability in this field, is wholly neutral in its effects, or can sometimes become an outright hindrance. Certain experiments have shown that the automatic recording processes of our visual memory achieve the same result as systematic lessons: in two groups of students, of which one had been given spelling instruction and one had not, there was no difference between the two sets of marks. That particular experiment is still, no doubt, insufficient, since it lacked the necessary extension and variations. But it is scarcely believable that in a field so accessible to experiment, and one in which the divergent interests of traditional grammar and contemporary linguistic theory are in such direct conflict, that the pedagogue has not organized sustained and methodical experiments, but has remained content to decide upon such questions on the basis of opinions whose "common sense" in fact conceals more affectivity than effective reasoning.

In fact, all we have at our disposal as a basis for judging the productivity of our scholastic methods are the results of end-of-school examinations and, to some extent, certain competitive examinations. But the use of these data entails both a begging of the question and a vicious circle.

A begging of the question, to begin with, because we are postulating that success in those examinations constitutes a proof of durability of the knowledge acquired, whereas the real problem, still in no way resolved, consists precisely in attempting to establish what remains after a lapse of several years of the knowledge whose existence has been proved once by success in those examinations, as well as in trying to determine the exact composition of whatever still subsists independently of the detailed knowledge forgotten. On these two prime points, then, we still have almost no information.

A vicious circle, in the second place—and this is even more serious—because we are saying that it is possible to judge the value of
scholastic instruction by success in final examinations when the
fact is that a great deal of the work done in school is influenced by
the prospect of those very examinations, and is even seriously
distorted, according to some respected thinkers, as this preoccupa-
tion becomes increasingly dominant. It therefore goes without saying, if we are to achieve any scientific objectivity or even any hon-
esty with regard to the parents and above all the students involved,
that it must be a preliminary consideration of any pedagogical
study of scholastic productivity to compare the results of schools
without examinations, where the student's worth is evaluated by
the teachers as a function of work done throughout the year, with
those of ordinary schools where the prospect of final examinations
may be falsifying not only the work of the students but even that of
the teachers as well. It will be objected that the teachers will not
always be impartial in their evaluations; but would any conceivable
local partialities ever wreak as much havoc as the aleatory element
and the emotional blockage that are involved in every examination? It will also be objected that students are not mere guinea pigs
for us to use in pedagogical experiments; but are not the many
administrative decisions or reorganizations that occur at present
ultimately experiments, too, and different from scientific experiments only in that they include no systematic controls? And it will
also be objected, above all, that examinations may also fulfill a
formative function, etc.; but this is precisely what we ought to be
verifying with the help of objective experiments, refusing to remain
content with mere opinions, even when adorned with the authoritative label "according to the experts," especially since those opinions are both so numerous and so contradictory.

The fact is that on all these fundamental questions, as on many
others, too, experimental pedagogy—even though it does exist and
has already accomplished much valuable work—still remains si-
lent, thereby testifying to the terrifying disproportion that still subsists between the scope or importance of the problems facing it and
the means being employed to resolve them. When a doctor applies

a given therapy it is true that his decision to do so also involves a certain degree of empiricism, and one can never be entirely certain with any particular case whether it is the remedies employed that have led to a cure or whether the *vis medicatrix naturae* would have achieved it in any case, without outside help. But there does nevertheless exist a considerable body of pharmacological and other research which, combined with our progress in physiological knowledge, provides an increasingly solid foundation for clinical intuitions. How is it, then, that in the field of pedagogy, one in which the future of the next few generations is as much involved as in the field of health, basic research should have remained as meager as these few small examples indicate?

Research and the Teaching Body

In the period between 1935 and 1965, in almost all the branches of what we term the natural, social, or human sciences, one could quote the names of great writers, men of international reputation, who have revolutionized, more or less profoundly, the branches of learning to which they have devoted their labors. Yet, during that same period, no great pedagogue has appeared whom we can add to the list of eminent men whose names provide our milestones in the history of education. And this raises still another problem.

It is a problem, however, whose terms are not limited to the period in question. If we glance through the tables of contents in the various histories of education, the first observation inevitably thrust upon us is the very large proportion of innovators in the field of pedagogy who were not professional educators. Comenius created and ran schools, but he was by training a theologian and a philosopher. Rousseau never held classes, and though he may have had children we know that he did not occupy himself with them to any extent. Froebel, the creator of kindergartens and the champion of a sensory education (however inadequate it may have been) was a chemist and a philosopher. Herbart was a psychologist and a philosopher. Among our contemporaries, Dewey was a philosopher, Mme Montessori, Decroly, and Claparède were all doctors of medicine, and the latter two were psychologists as well. Pestalozzi, on the other hand, perhaps the most illustrious of the pedagogues who were purely and simply educators (though he was a very modern one), invented nothing in the way of new methods or approaches, unless we allow him the use of slates, and even that was simply for reasons of economy. . . .

One of the important events in pedagogy between 1935 and 1965 was the French project of reforms that gave rise to the "observation and guidance phases," which sprang directly from the work of a commission guided and inspired by a physicist and a psychologist-doctor (Langevin and Wallon).

There have doubtless been examples in other disciplines, too, of fundamental inspirations being contributed by men who were not "of the profession": everyone knows how much medicine, for example, is indebted to Pasteur, who was not a doctor. But medicine in its broad outline is nevertheless the work of doctors, the engineering sciences have been constructed by engineers, and so forth. So why is pedagogy so little the work of pedagogues? This is a serious and ever-present problem. The absence or scarcity of research on the results of scholastic instruction that we were emphasizing a moment ago is only one particular case. The general problem is to understand why the vast army of educators now laboring throughout the entire world with such devotion and, in general, with such competence, does not engender an elite of researchers capable of making pedagogy into a discipline, at once scientific and alive, that could take its rightful place among all those other applied disciplines that draw upon both art and science.

Is the reason inherent in the nature of pedagogy itself, in the sense that its lacunae are a direct effect of the impossibility of achieving a stable equilibrium between its scientific data and its social applications? That is something we shall go into later, in the light of the fresh problems that have arisen between 1935 and 1965. We shall answer in the negative, but before examining the theoretical questions it is indispensable to begin by giving due importance to the sociological factors, since it is as true in this case as in every other that a science cannot develop other than as a function of the needs and stimuli of a social environment. And the fact is that in this particular case those stimuli are to some extent lacking, and the environment not always favorable.

One phenomenon, the seriousness of which cannot escape notice and that has been becoming more and more clearly apparent during recent years, is the difficulty of recruiting primary and secondary schoolteachers. The XXVIth International Conference of Public Education placed on its agenda in 1963 the problem of "the struggle against the scarcity of primary teachers," and it became quite clear on that occasion how general the problem is. This, of course, is above all an economic question, and if we were able to grant teachers salaries equivalent to those earned by representatives of the other liberal professions, we should thereby increase the rate of recruitment. But the problem is much wider and in fact concerns the educator's position in social life as a whole: that is why it is so closely linked to our central question of pedagogical research.

The truth is that the profession of educator has not yet attained, in our societies, the normal status to which it has the right in the scale of intellectual values. A lawyer, even one of no exceptional talent, owes the consideration in which he is held to a respected and respectable discipline, that is, the law, whose prestige corresponds to clearly defined ranks among university teachers. A doctor, even one who does not always cure his patients, represents a hallowed science, the acquisition of which is a lengthy and arduous process. An engineer, like the doctor, represents a science and a technique. A university teacher represents the science he teaches and to whose progress he devotes his efforts. What the schoolteacher lacks, in contrast to all these, is a comparable intellectual prestige. And the reason for this lack is an extraordinary and rather disturbing combination of circumstances.

The general reason is, for the most part, that the schoolteacher is not thought of, either by others or, what is worse, by himself, as a specialist from the double point of view of techniques and scientific creativeness, but rather as the mere transmitter of a kind of knowledge that is within everyone's grasp. In other words, it is considered that a good teacher is providing what is expected of him when he is in possession of a general elementary education and has learned a few appropriate formulas that enable him to inculcate a similar education in the minds of his pupils.

Thinking in this way, it is very easy to forget that teaching in all its forms raises three central problems whose solutions are still far from being found, and of which we are still even bound to ask ourselves if they ever will be solved except with the collaboration of our teachers or of at least a section of them:

(1) What is the aim of this teaching? To accumulate useful knowledge (but useful in what sense?)? To teach students to learn? To teach students to innovate, to produce something new in whatever field is concerned, as well as to know? To teach how to check, to verify, or simply to repeat? And so forth.

(2) Once these aims have been selected (and by whom, or with whose consent?), it then remains to determine which branches (or sub-branches) are necessary, irrelevant, or contraindicated for the attainment of them: branches of education, branches of reasoning, and above all (something that still remains absent in a great many programs), branches of experimentation that will help to form a spirit of discovery and active verification.

(3) The appropriate branches selected, it remains lastly to acquire sufficient knowledge of the laws of mental development to be able to find the methods most suited to the type of educational formation desired.

We shall, of course, return to each of these problems—the position of which has been perceptibly modified since 1935—but the question for the moment is that of the situation of the teaching body with regard to research, and of the social obstacles that prevent teachers from engaging in such research into fundamental educational problems.

The first of these obstacles is that the public (which includes certain educational authorities and an appreciable number of the teachers themselves), being unaware of the complexity of these problems, does not know that pedagogy is a science comparable with other sciences, and even a very difficult one, given the complexity of the factors involved. When medicine applies biology and general physiology to the problems of curing diseases it need not

hesitate about the aims to be attained, and it employs the already
advanced sciences while itself collaborating in the development of
the intermediary disciplines (human physiology, pathology, phar-
macodynamics, etc.). In contrast, when pedagogy seeks to apply
the data of psychology and sociology, it finds itself confronted with
a tangle of questions concerning not only ends but also means, and
it receives no more than modest aid from its mother sciences, since
those disciplines have themselves still not made sufficient progress, and it has still to constitute its body of specific kinds of
knowledge (an educational psychology that is more than a merely
deductively applied child psychology, an experimental didactics,
etc.).

In the second place, the schoolteacher is constrained to conform
to a set program and apply the methods dictated to him by the state
(except in certain countries such as, in principle, Great Britain),
whereas the doctor, for example, is answerable more to his faculty
and to his professional council than to a ministry of health or hy-
giene. It is doubtless true that ministries of education are mainly
staffed by educators, but they are educators filling administrative
posts and therefore have no time to devote to research. And it is
also doubtless true that such ministries often take the precaution
of founding and consulting research institutes (such as the
pedagogical academies in Eastern countries together with the many
laboratories attached to them), but this still does not alter the fact
that the specific intellectual autonomy of the teaching body itself
still remains extremely restricted, throughout the world, in comparison with that enjoyed by the other liberal professions.

In the third place, if we compare the societies formed by educators to those formed by the medical or legal professions, to societies of engineers or architects, etc., in other words to all those professional associations within which the representatives of the same
discipline—even though they are "applied" disciplines as opposed
to the so-called pure sciences—engage in shared study projects or
exchange discoveries, one cannot but be struck by the prevailing
lack of scientific dynamism in these bodies of frequently specialized
educators when discussing exclusively intra-union problems.

In the fourth place, and this is doubtless the essential consideration, there are still many countries in which the training of teachers has no connection at all with university faculties: secondary-school teachers alone are trained at the university, and even then almost exclusively from the point of view of the subject they are going to teach, their pedagogic training properly speaking being either nonexistent or reduced to an absolute minimum, while primary-school teachers are trained separately in teacher training colleges that lack entirely any direct link with university research. We shall return later to the changes in ideas and institutions in this respect during the past thirty years, but it is important to note at this point what a deadly effect the traditional system has had upon educational research: first of all, it has left future secondary teachers in ignorance of the possibilities of such research (when it could produce such very fruitful results in secondary education in the fields, among others, of mathematics, physics, and linguistics). And secondly, it has helped to make the teaching body of the primary schools into a sort of introverted intellectual class apart, deprived of its rightful social recognition, a situation made worse by the fact that primary teachers are thereby cut off from the scientific trends and the atmosphere of research and experiment that could have injected new life into them had they been brought into contact with university teaching. (This problem will be taken up again in Chapter 8.)

Research Institutes

The remedy for the various situations just described has been sought, first of all, and rightly so, in the creation of institutes for educational research, a great many of which have sprung into being in recent years. This trend has become so widespread, in fact, that the International Bureau of Education has been able to undertake a comparative inquiry into the subject, and to hold a discussion on it at one of its international conferences on public education.

These institutions fall into three main types: the academies of educational science so much esteemed in the peoples' republics of the East, the institutes of educational science or education departments attached to universities in the form of faculties, departments,

or interfaculty institutes, and the research centers, whether officially recognized or not, operating independently of academies or
universities (museums of education, etc.).

The pedagogical academies constitute a model of organized research, generously financed by the state and permitting their researchers adequate autonomy in the details of their work (almost
the only restriction they find irksome, a fairly common one, is that
of being obliged to present research projects planned several years
ahead, which often introduces a somewhat artificial element into
their work, given the unpredictable nature of the research itself).
There are a considerable number of child psychologists in these institutions, each with a laboratory and assistants at his disposal, and
the result is a fairly close collaboration in the detailed study of
pedagogical problems. For example, in Moscow I was shown the
results of research that consisted in measuring perceptions (invari-
ables, etc.) in activity and play situations in order to compare them
with measurements taken in other contexts, the aim being to demonstrate the effects of activity and interest on perception itself: the
choice of such a line of investigation testifies at the same time to a
concern with the relating of research to general problems of importance for pedagogy and also to a certain independence with regard
to immediate applications that might limit the field of inquiries. But
it goes without saying that a considerable number of other research
projects bear upon the detailed questions of teaching itself, and the
results of these are passed on to practicing educators. Those
involved are, generally speaking, satisfied with systems like this, the
adjustments desired being reducible in the main to two: coordination between the work of the academies and that of the universities,
and coordination between the processes of practical research and
the training of the teachers themselves, which is at the moment still
entrusted to pedagogical institutes entirely separate from the research centers.

The second type of institution carrying out research is that
which exists within the universities, where the teachers whose task
it is to teach the various branches of pedagogy are expected, as in
all the other fields, not merely to teach courses in the subject but

also to organize research projects. Certain universities—and this became quite a widespread trend a few years ago—have created Faculties of Pedagogy or Education to rank with those of Letters, Sciences, or Social Science, etc. But the notorious drawbacks of the faculty system (which tends to compartmentalize knowledge and obstruct the interdisciplinary lines of communication that are vital for the development of certain branches of knowledge) are even more flagrant in the sphere of education than in others: the essential problems of pedagogical research are, in fact, to fertilize it by means of links with other disciplines and to draw the researchers out of isolation, or even to cure them of their inferiority feelings. Consequently, when the Institut J. J. Rousseau was attached to the University of Geneva (final stage in 1948) it refused the offer of being constituted as a separate faculty and chose instead the form of an inter-faculty institute, dependent upon the Faculty of Sciences for psychology (experimental psychology remaining with that faculty and the branches of child psychology and applied psychology being taken over by the institute) and upon the Faculty of Letters for pedagogy (the main chair remaining with that faculty and the subsidiary chairs being taken over by the institute). It is possible that this formula for inter-faculty institutes has some future in the sphere of other disciplines, and it is to be noted that it has been adopted by the University of Amsterdam as a means of coordinating all its philosophical studies.

Another form of link between pedagogical research and university life is that corresponding to the Anglo-Saxon systems in which the functional unit is constituted as a "department" rather than as a faculty. In such cases we find a Department of Education on the same footing as Departments of Psychology, and so forth. One could name many such Departments of Education, both in Great Britain and the United States, that are very much alive and provide much fine research. The members of such departments, however, do occasionally complain of two disadvantages. The first is the split that is introduced between psychology and pedagogy. This is often remedied by grouping child psychology together with pedagogy, but that has the defect of separating genetic psychology from experimental psychology (which has often had a somewhat disastrous effect) without providing a sufficient insurance against the Department of Education's possible isolation. The other disadvántage, alluded to with discretion, is the possibility this system offers for mathematicians, physicists, and biologists who have not been able in their own fields to find outlets in the Departments of Education for teaching the didactics of mathematics, physics, biology, and so on—a state of affairs that is not always of great advantage to the progress of pedagogical research.

Generally speaking, these various formulas for attaching pedagogical research to the universities have certainly shown themselves to be fruitful, and particularly insofar as they have succeeded in integrating the teaching body into the structures of higher education, a result achieved thanks to various methods of training teachers in the university itself, a subject we shall return to in Chapter 8.

As for the research centers that are independent of academies and universities, they too can be very effective. Some are officially recognized (educational museums, etc.) and sometimes have greater access to the ears of ministries than do the universities. Others, as in the United States, are dependent upon private foundations and may consequently offer a remarkable fluidity, as in the case of several "projects" concerned with the teaching of science from the most elementary stages onward. Under the influence of various events, from which the "Sputnik" should perhaps not be excluded, certain celebrated physicists, for example, have become keenly interested in the methods of acquiring certain modes of thinking, a development that must be accounted wholly profitable from the point of view of pedagogy.

Scientific Pedagogy and the Determination of the Aims of Education

It goes without saying that it is society's task to fix the aims of the education it is providing for its rising generations; and society, moreover, always does precisely that, all-powerfully and in two ways. It fixes them firstly, and spontaneously, by means of the restrictions imposed by language, customs, opinion, the family, economic necessities, etc., which is to say by means of all the many forms of collective action that societies usually employ to maintain and transform themselves, by modeling each new generation in the static or mobile matrix of the preceding ones. And it fixes them secondly, in a conscious way, through the organs of the state or by means of private institutions, in accordance with the types of education envisaged.

But this determination of educational ends does not take place haphazardly. Even when it is accomplished spontaneously it obeys sociological laws that can be analyzed, and such analyses can serve to enlighten the considered decisions made by the authorities in educational matters. As for those decisions themselves, they are not generally taken except as a result of information of all kinds, not only political but also economic, technical, moral, intellectual, and so forth. This information, generally speaking, is collected only by means of direct consultation with those involved, and this initial method of procedure is without doubt indispensable, as, for example, where the technical and economic needs of society are involved. But here once more it is extremely desirable that those responsible for issuing directives to the educators should be in possession of objective studies on the relation between social life and education. This means, on the one hand, that it is not enough to determine the ends in order to attain them, for there still remains the problem of means, which is a matter for psychology more than for sociology, but which nevertheless conditions the choice of ends. Consequently, Durkheim was simplifying things a little too much when he maintained that the man education is trying to create is a product of society and not of nature: the fact remains that nature does not submit to the wishes of society except upon certain conditions, and that by acquiring a knowledge of them instead of thwarting them, one achieves enlightenment on one's choice of social goals. On the other hand, limiting ourselves to the matter of goals, the various finalities desired may be more or less mutually compatible or contradictory: it is not proved, for example, that we can expect the individuals we train to be constructors and innovators in certain spheres of social activity, where such qualities are needed, and at the same time rigorous conformists in other branches of knowledge and activity. So that either the determination of the goals of education must remain a matter of "authorized" opinion and empiricism, or else it must be the object of systematic study. This choice has become progressively more evident in recent years.

We have therefore seen the development of a sociology of education that has somewhat neglected (though this trend will be reversed) the great problems discussed by the founders of this discipline, Durkheim and Dewey, but has specialized in the study of concrete structures—for example, the study of the school class as a group possessing its own peculiar dynamics (sociometry, efficient communications between teachers and students, etc.), the study of the teaching body as a social category (recruitment, hierarchic structures, ideology, etc.), and, above all, the study of the student population: social origin of students in relation to levels attained, career opportunities, bottlenecks, social mobility in relation to educational factors, etc.

The problems relating to the student population have most captured attention and are effectively the most important insofar as judging the goals of teaching is concerned. The "economics of education" is one of the fields that is beginning to experience great developments: a study of the coincidences and discrepancies existing between educational systems and the economic and "social" needs of society as a whole, the nature and amplitude of the resources put at the school's disposal, the productivity of particular systems, the relationships between the guidance given to young people in school, and the developments occurring in various forms of economic activity, etc.

It goes without saying that this kind of work as a whole is of fairly central importance for "educational planning," which is a matter of interest in almost every country today and which consists in drawing up reform projects for many years ahead. Such planning is, of course, linked to a determination of the goals to be aimed at, and such a determination could certainly shed varying degrees of light on certain areas of the sociology of education.

It will be objected that the information necessary for the planning and fixing of our educational aims could be derived more directly from the work on comparative education carried out by so many people in the United States (Kandel, etc.) and Great Britain (Lauwerys, etc.), and still being pursued at the International Bureau of Education by P. Rossello in research based on the annual reports of the ministries of public education recorded in the *International Yearbook of Education and Teaching*. By comparing the quantifiable items of information in particular, it is possible to isolate certain trends according to the increases or diminutions from one year to another, or certain correlations in terms of the interdependence of problems. But it must be clearly understood that comparative education has no future unless it is kept resolutely subordinated to sociology, that is, to a detailed and systematic study of the social conditioning of the various educational systems. And it must also be realized that no quantitative study, in itself an extremely delicate matter because we lack units of measurement (hence the "ordinal" methods with all the precautions they presuppose), has any significance unless it is subordinated to qualitative analyses, a fact that brings us back to the great problems that cannot be avoided.

Experimental Pedagogy or
the Study of Programs and Methods

Whether educational programs and teaching methods are imposed by the state or left to the initiative of teachers, it is still quite clear that we can make no justified statements about their practical productivity, or, above all, about the numerous unexpected effects they may have upon the general formation of individuals, without systematic study employing all the means so fertile in possibilities for cross-checking that have been developed by modern statistical science and the various fields of psychosociological research.

Several decades ago, as a result of this realization, a new discipline was constituted called "experimental pedagogy" whose task was the specialized study of such problems. Claparède, in a work bearing the double title *Psychologie de l'enfant et pédagogie experimentale* that went into numerous editions and was much translated at the beginning of this century, had already shown that this experimental pedagogy is not a branch of psychology (except in that it integrates all the activities of teachers themselves into the subject matter of the latter science). Experimental pedagogy is concerned, in practice, solely with the development and the results of pedagogic processes proper, which does not mean, as we shall see, that psychology does not constitute a necessary reference for it, but that the problems posed are different from those of psychology, and that they are concerned less with the general and spontaneous characteristics of the child and its intelligence than with their modification by the process in question.

It is, for example, a question for experimental pedagogy to decide whether the best way of learning to read consists in beginning with the letters, then graduating to words and finally to sentences, in accordance with the classical or "analytical" method, or whether it is better to work through these stages in reverse order, in accordance with Decroly's "total" method. Only a patient, methodical research program, using comparable groups of subjects for equally comparable periods of time, while taking care to neutralize as far as possible any adventitious factors (quality of the teachers and their preferences for one or other method, etc.) can permit a solution of the question; and there can be no question of seeking for a solution by means of deductive considerations based upon knowledge provided by psychology, however experimental in origin itself, about the role of "gestalts" in our perception, or about the syncretic or total character of perception in the child (even though it was such considerations that led Decroly to conceive and create his method, since that in itself does not constitute verification). Certain studies of this subject, though still far from complete, have led to claims that the total method, though it produces results more swiftly, is harmful to the child's grasp of spelling later on; but this claim is merely the result of random observations requiring another set of extremely delicate controls. (One has only to think of the many adults who, when hesitating between two possible spellings, write out the word in question in both forms and choose according

to the resulting appearances, a process that consists, in fact, in recognizing correct spelling with relation to a total visual configuration.) Other research has seemed to show that the results obtained
vary according to the types of children involved and above all according to the types of activities with which the "total" exercises
are associated in practice, a fact that has recently led a woman
educator at Sherbrooke in Canada to develop a mixed method, one
that is mainly total but in which the children themselves cooperate
in the construction of sentences by selecting possible combinations
of words contributed by each member of the group. The outcome
of this is the need for yet further research and controls that will
take this third possibility into account and establish a basis for
comparison between it and the others. Certain authors have maintained recently that the problem must always remain badly posed if
we limit ourselves to the perceptual and mnemonic factors, and
that the real question must be situated at the level of meanings and
of the interplay of relationships between signs and that which is
signified, etc.; and if such a point of view is adopted, then a whole
range of new experiments is opened up for experimental pedagogy,
one that does not moreover exclude in any way the necessity for
correlation with perceptual factors, since though these latter are
not the only factors concerned, that does not mean they have become negligible.

This commonplace example demonstrates, in the first place, the
complexity of the problems confronting experimental pedagogy if
we wish to judge educational methods according to objective criteria and not merely according to the evaluations of them made by
the teachers involved, by inspectors, or by the students' parents. It
further shows that the problems are, in reality, of a pedagogical
order and not purely psychological, since the measurement of scholastic productivity obeys criteria that are the concern of the educator alone, even if the methods employed do partly overlap with
those of the psychologist. On the other hand, the question of the
necessity for collaboration between experimental pedagogy and
child psychology as against the desirability of a radical independ

ence for the former has also been raised in recent years, particularly in French-speaking pedagogical circles.

This problem has not arisen, however, either in the Anglo-Saxon countries or in the peoples' republics, where it is tacitly accepted in all the research centers that are dependent upon universities and in the pedagogical academies that experimental pedagogy is bound to rely upon psychology in much the same way as medicine relies upon biology or physiology, while remaining distinct from them. In direct contrast, R. Dottrens, backed by the Association of Experimental Pedagogy in French-speaking countries, which he has helped to create, maintains the necessity for complete independence on the part of that discipline, and in order to defend this point of view, he has, rather curiously, invoked texts by Claparède that merely indicate the differences of the problems involved, as though the entire work of the founder of the Institut J. J. Rousseau had not been directed toward settling pedagogy upon solid psychological foundations. In fact, the problem is extremely simple, and its solution depends solely on how modest or how wide the ambitions of experimental pedagogy are.

If it intends to limit itself, in conformity with the positivist conception of science, to a simple investigation into facts and laws, without claiming to explain what it states, then naturally there is no need whatever for a connection with psychology. It will be observed, for example, that in three comparable groups of young children the analytical method produced after x months an ability to read an average of n words in 150 minutes, the total method produced n' words, and the Sherbrooke method n'' words, using the same text. Meanwhile the rapidity of the progress made month by month will also be measured. Lastly, it will be observed that after two or three years these same groups, having received identical instruction in other respects, will have produced such and such results with regard to spelling ability. And that will be the end of it, the most to be expected as a result being a possibility of choosing among the methods discussed.

But if experimental pedagogy wishes to understand what it is doing and to complete its observations with causal interpretations or "explanations," it is obvious that it will have to employ a precise psychology, not merely that of common sense. In the case of our present example it will have to possess detailed information in the fields of visual perception, and the perception of words, letters, and sentences; it will have to know exactly what the relations are between total perception and the "perceptual activities," as well as the laws of symbolic function, the relationships between word perception and symbolism, etc.

And the example selected is in no way exceptional. Any didactic method or any program of instruction, if its application and results are to be analyzed by experimental pedagogy, will raise problems pertaining to the psychology of development, the psychology of learning, and the general psychology of intelligence. Consequently, any advances to be made by experimental pedagogy, taken as an independent science with regard to its subject matter, must necessarily be linked, as in all sciences, to interdisciplinary researches, if there is to be any question of constituting it as a true science–of its being, in other words, not merely descriptive but explanatory. This, moreover, is a fact that the immense majority of research centers in this young discipline have understood, and what I have just said is really no more than an enunciation of what has become a generally accepted truth during recent years.

2. Advances in Child and Adolescent Psychology

Introduction

Volume XV of the *Encyclopédie Française* contains a chapter by myself, written more than thirty years ago, on what child psychology has to offer the educator. Comparing those pages with the article contributed by H. Wallon to volume VIII, which was devoted to the "Life of the Mind," L. Febvre thought he could discern a certain divergence between the two that might be of interest to pedagogy, Wallon insisting above all on the gradual incorporation of children into the social life organized by the adult, and myself emphasizing above all the spontaneous and relatively autonomous aspects of the development of children's intellectual structures.

Although Wallon's psychology and my own have ultimately become much more complementary than antagonistic, because his analysis of thought elucidates above all its figurative aspects while mine emphasizes its operative aspects (a point I have attempted to make clear in my *Hommage à H. Wallon,* a short article that appeared after that friend's regretted death but about which he was given the time to write to me, approving of this "dialectical reconciliation"), the problem raised by L. Febvre still remains undiminished today, even though it now poses itself in terms that have been modified by a considerable body of facts discovered since that time.

This problem, a more or less central one where the choice of teaching methods is concerned, presents itself in practice in the following terms: there are some subjects, such as French history or spelling, whose contents have been developed, or even invented, by adults, and the transmission of which raises no problems other than those related to recognizing the better or worse information techniques. There are other branches of learning, on the other hand, characterized by a mode of truth that does not depend upon more or less particular events resulting from many individual decisions, but upon a process of research and discovery during the course of which the human intelligence affirms its own existence and its properties of universality and autonomy: a mathematical truth is not dependent upon the contingencies of adult society but upon a rational construction accessible to any healthy intelligence; an elementary truth in physics is verifiable by an experimental process that is similarly not dependent upon collective opinions but upon a rational approach, both inductive and deductive, equally accessible to that same healthy intelligence. The problem, then, where truths of this type are concerned, is to decide whether they are better acquired by means of educational methods of transmission analogous to that which is more or less successful in the case of knowledge of the first type, or whether a truth is never truly assimilated as a truth except insofar as it has first been reconstructed or rediscovered by means of some activity adequate to that task.

Such was the cardinal problem of contemporary pedagogy in 1935, and it remains so today. If we desire, in answer to what is becoming an increasingly widely felt need, to form individuals capable of inventive thought and of helping the society of tomorrow to achieve progress, then it is clear that an education which is an active discovery of reality is superior to one that consists merely in providing the young with ready-made wills to will with and ready-made truths to know with. Though, even if one is setting out to train conformist minds that will keep to the already mapped out paths of accepted truths, the question remains one of determining whether the transmission of established truths is more efficiently carried out by using processes of simple repetition or by a more active form of assimilation.

And, in fact, it is to this problem, though without having deliberately set out to solve it, that child psychology, having developed to such an extent since 1935, is now able to give a more complete answer than before. And this answer bears on three points in particular, all three of them of decisive importance with regard to the choice of didactic methods and even to the working out of educational programs: the nature of intelligence or knowledge, the role of experience in the formation of ideas, and the mechanism of social or linguistic communications between adult and child.

The Formation of the Intelligence and the Active Nature of Knowledge

In an article written recently for the *Encyclopedia Britannica,* R. M. Hutchins affirms that the principal aim of education is to develop the intelligence itself, and above all to teach how to develop it "for as long as it is capable of further progress," which is to say, of course, far beyond the age at which one leaves school. Whether the ends allotted to education, either openly or in secret, consist in subordinating the individual to society as it is or working toward a better society, everyone will doubtless accept Hutchins' formula. But it is also quite clear that this formula does not mean very much unless one can be quite precise about what intelligence consists of, for although the notions of common sense on this subject are as uniform as they are inexact, those of the theoreticians vary sufficiently to inspire the most divergent forms of pedagogy. It is therefore indispensable to consult the facts in order to find out what intelligence is, and psychological experiment has no means of answering that question other than by characterizing that intelligence according to its modes of formation and development. Fortunately, however, it is precisely in this field that child psychology has provided us with most new results since 1935.

The essential functions of intelligence consist in understanding and in inventing, in other words in building up structures by structuring reality. It increasingly appears, in fact, that these two functions are inseparable, since, in order to understand a phenomenon or an event, we must reconstitute the transformations of which they are the resultant, and since, also, in order to reconstitute them, we must have worked out a structure of transformations, which presupposes an element of invention or of reinvention. Whereas the older theories of intelligence (empirical associationism, etc.) emphasized understanding (even to the extent of assimilating it to a process of reduction from the complex to the simple, in accordance with an atomistic model in which sensation, the image, and association were assigned the essential roles) and looked upon invention as the mere discovery of already existing realities, more recent theories, on the other hand, increasingly verified by facts, subordinate understanding to invention, looking upon the latter as the expression of a continual construction process building up structured wholes.

The problem of intelligence, and with it the central problem of the pedagogy of teaching, has thus emerged as linked with the fundamental epistemological problem of the nature of knowledge: does the latter constitute a copy of reality or, on the contrary, an assimilation of reality into a structure of transformations? The ideas behind the knowledge-copy concept have not been abandoned by everyone, far from it, and they continue to provide the inspiration for many educational methods, even, quite often, for those intuitive methods in which the image and audio-visual presentations play a role that certain people tend to look upon as the ultimate triumph of educational progress. In child psychology, many authors continue to think that the formation of the intelligence obeys the laws of "learning," after the model of certain Anglo-Saxon theories of learning exemplified by those of Hull: repeated responses of the organism to external stimuli, consolidation of those repetitions by external reinforcements, constitution of chains of association or of a "hierarchy of habits" which produce a "functional copy" of the regular sequences of reality, and so forth.

But the essential fact that contradicts these survivals of associationist empiricism, the establishing of which has revolutionized our concepts of intelligence, is that knowledge is derived from action, not in the sense of simple associative responses, but in the much deeper sense of the assimilation of reality into the necessary and general coordinations of action. To know an object is to act upon it and to transform it, in order to grasp the mechanisms of that transformation as they function in connection with the transformative actions themselves. To know is therefore to assimilate reality into structures of transformation, and these are the structures that intelligence constructs as a direct extension of our actions.

The fact that intelligence derives from action, an interpretation in conformity with the French-speaking psychological tradition of the past few decades, leads up to this fundamental consequence: even in its higher manifestations, when it can only make further progress by using the instruments of thought, intelligence still consists in executing and coordinating actions, though in an interiorized and reflexive form. These interiorized actions, which are still actions nevertheless insofar as they are processes of transformation, are nothing other than the logical or mathematical "operations" that are the motors of all judgment, or reasoning. But these operations are not just any interiorized actions, and they present, moreover, insofar as they are expressions of the most general coordinations of action, the double character of being reversible (every operation includes an inverse, as with addition and subtraction, or a reciprocal, etc.), and of coordinating themselves in consequence into larger total structures (a classification, the sequence of whole numbers, etc.). It follows from this that intelligence, at all levels, is an assimilation of the datum into structures of transformations, from the structures of elementary actions to the higher operational structures, and that these structurations consist in an organization of reality, whether in act or thought, and not in simply making a copy of it.

Development of Mental Operations

It is the continuous development, leading from initial sensorimotor actions to the most abstract mental operations, that child psychology has attempted to describe in the past thirty years, and the facts obtained in numerous countries, as well as their increasingly convergent interpretations, today provide those educators who wish to employ them with a number of sufficiently consistent elements of reference.

The origin of our intellectual operations is thus to be sought for as far back as an initial stage of the development characterized by sensorimotor actions and intelligence. With perceptions and movements as its only tools, without yet being capable of either representation or thought, this entirely practical intelligence nevertheless provides evidence, during the first years of our existence, of an effort to comprehend situations. It does, in practice, achieve the construction of schemata of action that will serve as substructures for the operational and notional structures built up later on. At this level, for example, we can already observe the construction of a fundamental schema of conservation, which is that of the permanence of solid objects, these being looked for from nine to ten months onward (after essentially negative phases in this respect) behind screens cutting them off from any actual perceptual field. Correlatively, we can also observe the formation of structures that are already almost reversible, such as the organization of the displacements and positions within a "grouping" characterized by the possibility of forward and backward or circling movements (reversible mobility). We can watch the formation of causal relationships, linked first of all to the action proper alone, then progressively objectified and spatialized through connection with the construction of the object, of space, and of time. One of the facts that helps to verify the importance of this sensorimotor schematism for the formation of future mental operations is that in those born blind, as we know from the research of Y. Hatwell, the inadequacy of the initial schemata leads to a lag in development of three to four years and more in the formation of the more general operations, and lasting until adolescence, whereas children who become blind at a later age suffer a much less considerable retardation.

At about the age of two, a second period lasting until the seventh or eighth year begins. The onset of this second period is marked by the formation of the symbolic or semiotic function. This enables us to represent objects or events that are not at the moment perceptible by evoking them through the agency of symbols or differentiated signs. Symbolic play is an example of this process, as are deferred imitation, mental images, drawing, etc., and, above all, language itself. The symbolic function thus enables the sensorimotor intelligence to extend itself by means of thought, but there exist, on the other hand, two circumstances that delay the formation of mental operations proper, so that during the whole of this second period intelligent thought remains preoperational.

The first of these circumstances is the time that it takes to interiorize actions as thought, since it is much more difficult to represent the unfolding of an action and its results to oneself in terms of thought than to limit oneself to a material execution of it: for example, to impose a rotation on a square in thought alone, while representing to oneself every ninety degrees the position of the variously colored sides, is quite different from turning the square physically and observing the effects. The interiorization of actions thus presupposes their reconstruction at a new level, and this reconstruction may pass through the same stages as the previous reconstruction of the action itself, but with a much greater time lag.

In the second place, this reconstruction presupposes a continual decentering process that is much broader in scope than on the sensorimotor level. During his first two years of development (the sensorimotor period), the child has already been obliged to accomplish a sort of Copernican revolution in little: having begun by bringing all things back to its own body, it has ended by constituting a causal and spatiotemporal universe such that its own body is no longer considered as just one more object among others, all existing within an immense network of relationships that is beyond its grasp. On the level of reconstructions in thought the same holds true, but on a much broader scale, and with another difficulty added: the child must situate himself not only in relation to the totality of things, but also in relation to the totality of people around him, which presupposes a decentering process that is simultaneously relational and also social, and therefore a transition from egocentrism to those two forms of coordination, the sources of operational reversibility (inversions and reciprocities).

Lacking mental operations, the child cannot succeed during this second period in constituting the most elementary notions of conservation, which are the conditions of logical deductibility. Thus he imagines that ten counters arranged in a row become greater in number when the spaces between them are increased; that a collection of objects divided in two becomes quantitatively greater than the initial whole; that a straight line represents a greater distance if it is broken in two; that the distance between A and B is not necessarily the same as that between B and A (especially if there is a slope); that a quantity of liquid in glass A increases when poured into the narrower glass B, etc.

At about seven or eight years of age, however, there begins a third period in which these problems and many others are easily resolved because of the growing interiorization, coordinating, and decentering processes, which result in that general form of equilibrium constituted by operational reversibility (inversions and reciprocities). In other words, we are watching the formation of mental operations: linking and dissociation of classes, the sources of classification; the linking of relations $A < B < C$ . . . the source of seriation; correspondences, the sources of double entry tables, etc.; synthesis of inclusions in classes and serial order, which gives rise to numbers; spatial divisions and ordered displacements, leading to a synthesis of them, which is mensuration, etc.

But these many budding operations still cover no more than a doubly limited field. On the one hand they are still applied solely to objects, not to hypotheses set out verbally in the form of propositions (hence the uselessness of lecturing to the younger classes in primary schools and the necessity for concrete teaching methods). And, on the other hand, they still proceed only from one thing to the one next to it, as opposed to later combinative and proportional operations, which possess a much greater degree of mobility. These two limitations have a certain interest and show in what way these initial operations, which we term "concrete," are still close to the action from which they derive, since the linkages, seriations, correspondences, etc., carried out in the form of physical actions also effectively present these two types of characteristics.

Finally, at about eleven to twelve years of age, there begins a fourth and final period of which the plateau of equilibrium coincides with adolescence. This period is characterized in general by the conquest of a new mode of reasoning, one that is no longer limited exclusively to dealing with objects or directly representable realities, but also employs "hypotheses," in other words, propositions from which it is possible to draw logical conclusions without it being necessary to make decisions about their truth or falsity before examining the result of their implications. We are thus seeing the formation of new operations, which we term "propositional," in addition to the earlier concrete operations: implications ("if . . . then"), disjunctions ("either . . . or"), incompatibilities, conjunctions, etc. And these operations present two new fundamental characteristics. In the first place, they entail a combinative process, which is not the case with the "groupings" of classes and relationships at the previous level, and this combinative process is applied from the very first to objects or physical factors as well as to ideas and propositions. In the second place, each proportional operation corresponds to an inverse and to a reciprocal, so that these two forms of reversibility, dissociated until this point (inversion of classes only, reciprocity of relationships only) are from now on joined to form a total system in the form of a group of four transformations.

The Figurative and Operative Aspects of Knowledge

The spontaneous development of the intelligence, which leads from elementary sensorimotor actions through to concrete and then to formal operations, is thus characterized by the progressive establishment of systems of transformations or conversions. We shall call this aspect of knowledge "operative," the term embracing the initial actions as well as the operative structures proper (in the strict sense). But the realities to be known do not consist solely in "transformations" and consist equally of "states," since every transformation originates in one state in order to attain another, and since each state constitutes the product or the starting point of transformations. We shall term "figurative" the tools of knowledge that deal with states or that translate movements and transformations in terms of simple successions of states: perception, for instance, as well as imitation and that particular sort of interiorized imitation constituted by the mental image.

These, too, are points on which child psychology has provided new facts in the years since 1935 that are likely to interest the educator. Sensory education has, in fact, been given a great deal of attention since earliest times, and Froebel attempted to codify it for pre-scholastic levels. Periodically, emphasis is put on the role of "intuitive" methods, and it often happens that well-intentioned pedagogues imagine that the principal advantage of active methods is that of replacing abstraction by concrete contacts (even though, as we have just seen, there exists an "active" construction process for abstraction) and even believe they have attained the summit of educational progress by multiplying intuitive figurations in forms that no longer have anything active about them at all. It will therefore be of some pedagogic utility to examine how recent psychological research views the relationships between the figurative and the operative aspects of thought.

Where perception is concerned, first of all, it is increasingly difficult today to believe as we did once that ideas and operations are derived from perception by means of simple abstractions and generalizations. It is true that in 1954 Michotte tried to prove that the idea of cause originates in a "perception of causality," and we do in fact find this form of perception even in the very young child. But we have been able to show that sensorimotor causality does not derive from perceptive causality, and that, to the contrary, visual perceptive causality is based upon a tactico-kinesthesic causality that is itself dependent upon the activity proper as a whole, and is not exclusively upon perceptual factors. It follows from this that operational causality has its roots in sensorimotor causality and not in perceptive causality, since this latter is itself dependent upon sensorimotor causality in its motor as well in its perceptual aspects. This example is representative of many others: whenever it is be-lieved that an idea has been derived from a perception, without any other process intervening, in every case the activity itself has been forgotten, and it becomes apparent later that the sensorimotor activity constitutes the common origin of the corresponding ideas and perceptions. This is a general and fundamental fact that education cannot ignore.

As for representation by images, the facts studied testify equally to a constant subordination of the figurative aspects of thought to its operative aspects. By following the development of mental images in the child we observe, in effect, that in the preoperational stages the image remains astonishingly static, being limited to simple reproduction because of the child's inability to anticipate movements or the result of transformations: for example, the child of from four to six years envisages the conversion of an arc into a straight line by the tightening of a curved wire as producing a straight line equal to the substance (not daring to go beyond the frontiers represented by the ends of the initial arc) and as an abrupt transition, since it is unable to imagine the intermediate states. It is only under the influence of the budding concrete operations, at about seven to eight and beyond, that the image becomes both anticipatory and more mobile. The development of mental images does not therefore obey autonomous laws but presupposes the intervention of factors external to itself, which are operational in nature. Even in the sphere of image-recall and memory, it can be shown how much the structuration and even the conservation of the memories are linked to the schemata of actions and operations: for example, if we compare the memories that distinct groups of children retain of a grouping of cubes, according to whether the grouping has been (a) simply looked at or perceived, (b) recon-structed by the child itself, or (c) constructed by an adult while the child watches, we find that the memories produced by case (b) are clearly superior. The demonstration by an adult (c) produces no better results than simple perception (a), which shows once again that by carrying out experiments in the child's presence instead of making the child carry them out, one loses the entire informational and formative value offered by action proper as such.

Maturation and Exercise of the Intelligence

The development of intelligence, as it emerges from the recent research just described, is dependent upon natural, or spontaneous, processes, in the sense that they may be utilized and accelerated by education at home or in school but that they are not derived from that education and, on the contrary, constitute the preliminary and necessary condition of efficacity in any form of instruction. (See the oligophrenes in whom the very best forms of education are insufficient to produce the intelligence of which they have been deprived.) This spontaneity that characterizes the development of operational ability is attested to by the comparative studies that have been carried out in various countries (for example, the operations of conservation have been found in both illiterate Iranian country children and in deaf-mutes, the latter suffering a slight organizational retardation, but less than blind children).

It might therefore be supposed that intellectual operations constitute the expression of neural coordinations that develop as a function of organic maturation alone. Because the maturation of the nervous system is not completed until about the fifteenth or sixteenth year, it therefore seems evident that it does play a necessary role in the formation of mental structures, even though very little is known about that role.

The fact that a condition is necessary, however, does not mean that it is sufficient, and it is easy to show that the maturation of the organism is not the only factor at work in the development of operational ability: the maturation of the nervous system does no more than open up possibilities, excluded until particular age levels are reached, but it still remains to actualize them, and that presupposes other conditions, of which the most immediate is the functional exercise of the intelligence bound up with actions.

The proof of this limited character of the role of physical maturation is that, though the stages of development we have described always succeed one another in the same order, as do their substages, which is clear enough proof of the "natural" and spontaneous character of their sequential development (each one being necessary for the preparation of the following one and for the completion of the preceding one), they do not, on the other hand, correspond to absolute ages; on the contrary, accelerations or delays are observed according to differences of social environment and acquired experience. Canadian psychologists working in Martinique, for example, using my own operational tests, have discovered time lags of up to as much as four years in this respect, and in children whose primary school program is identical with that used in France.

The Factors of Acquired Experience

There has been an ever increasing emphasis during the past few years on a point that I feel can never be sufficiently stressed, which is that there exists a fundamental lacuna in our teaching methods, most of which, in a civilization very largely reliant upon the experimental sciences, continue to display an almost total lack of interest in developing the experimental attitude of mind in our students. It is therefore a matter of no little educational interest to examine what child psychology has been able to teach us in recent years about the role of acquired experience in the development of intelligence and about the development of spontaneous experimentation.

On the first point, we know today that experience is necessary to the development of intelligence, but that it is not sufficient in itself, and above all that it occurs in two very different forms between which classical empiricism failed to distinguish: physical experience and logico-mathematical experience.

Physical experience consists in acting upon objects and in discovering properties by abstraction from those objects: for example, weighing objects and observing that the heaviest are not always the largest. Logico-mathematical experience (indispensable during the stages at which operational deduction is still not possible) also consists in acting upon objects, but the processes of abstraction by which their properties are discovered are directed, not at the objects as such but at the actions that are brought to bear on the objects: for example, placing pebbles in a row and discovering that their number is the same whether we move from left to right or right to left (or in a circle, etc.); in this case, neither the order nor the numerical sum were properties of the pebbles before they were laid out or before they were counted, and the discovery that the sum is independent of the order (= interchangeability) consists in abstracting that observation from the actions of enumerating and ordering, even though the "reading" of the experiment was directed at the objects, since those properties of sum and order were in fact introduced into the objects by the actions.

As for physical experiment, that remains fairly simple-minded for a long while in the child, as indeed it did until the seventeenth century in the history of Western civilization itself, and consists at first merely in classifying objects and putting them into relationships or correspondence with one another by means of "concrete" operations, though without any systematic dissociation of the factors involved. This direct way of approaching reality, which is nearer to immediate experience than to experimentation proper, sometimes suffices to lead the experimenter to the discovery of certain causal relationships: for example, when at about seven or eight years the child comes to additive operations and the notions of conservation that spring from them, he will also come to understand that the sugar dissolved in a glass of water does not cease to exist, as he had at first thought, but is preserved in the forms of tiny invisible grains whose sum is equal to the total quantity of sugar cubes immersed, etc. But in the majority of cases concrete operations are insufficient for the analysis of phenomena. With propositional operations, on the other hand, and above all the combinativity they make possible, between the ages of eleven to twelve and fourteen to fifteen we find the formation of an experimental spirit: faced with a fairly complex phenomenon (flexibility, oscillations of a pendulum, etc.) the child seeks to dissociate the factors and to introduce variations into each one in isolation by neutralizing the others, or to make systematic combinations between them, etc. Our schools often have no idea of the possible developments to be achieved from such aptitudes, and we shall return later to the essential pedagogic problem raised by their existence.

Educational Communication and Equilibration

Apart from the factors of maturation and experiment, the acquisition of knowledge naturally depends upon educational or social communications (linguistics, etc.), and for a long while it was solely to this process that the traditional school confined its attention. Psychology in no way wishes to neglect such communication but sets itself to study questions that affect it and that may have been supposed to be long since resolved: does the success of such communication depend solely upon the quality of the presentation made by the adult himself of what he desires to inculcate in the child, or does it presuppose in the latter the presence of instruments of assimilation whose absence will prevent all comprehension?

As far as the action of experiment upon the development of knowledge is concerned, it has long since become commonplace to show how far the mind is from being a *tabula rasa* upon which ready-made connections may then be imprinted at the will of the external environment: it is observable, on the contrary, and recent researches have increasingly confirmed this, that all experiment necessitates a structuration of reality, in other words, that the recording of any external datum presupposes instruments of assimilation inherent in the activity of the subject. But when it is a question of adult speech, transmitting or seeking to transmit knowledge already structured by the language or the intelligence of the parents or the teachers themselves, then people may suppose preliminary assimilation to be sufficient, so that the child need do no more than incorporate this predigested intellectual nourishment as it is presented, as though the process of transmission did not require a fresh assimilation, in other words, a restructuration dependent this time upon the activities of the hearer. In a word, whenever it is a question of speech or verbal instruction, we tend to start off from the implicit postulate that this educational transmission supplies the child with the instruments of assimilation as such simultaneously with the knowledge to be assimilated, forgetting that such instruments cannot be acquired except by means of internal activity, and that all assimilation is a restructuration or a reinvention.

Recent researches have demonstrated this in the field of language itself. A child at the preoperational stage between five and six years, having observed the equality in length of two rulers when they are superimposed, will say that one of them is longer than the other if one of its ends is pushed out a few centimeters beyond its fellow, because the term "longer" is understood (notionally as well as semantically) in an ordinal and not a metric sense, and therefore in the sense of "reaching further." Similarly, faced with a series $A<B<C$, the child will say that A is little, C is big, and B is in between, but will have great difficulty in accepting that B is at the same time bigger than A and smaller than C, because the qualities of "bigness" and "littleness" are for a long while incompatible, etc. In a word, language is not sufficient to transmit a logic, and it is understood only thanks to logical instruments of assimilation whose origin lies much deeper, since they are dependent upon the general coordination of actions or of operations.

The main conclusions that the varied researches of child psychology have offered pedagogy in the last few years are thus related to the very nature of intellectual development. On the one hand, this development is essentially dependent upon the activities of the subject, and its constant mainspring, from pure sensorimotor activity through to the most completely interiorized operations, is an irreducible and spontaneous operativity. On the other hand, this operativity is neither preformed once and for all nor explicable solely by the external contributions of experiment or social transmission: it is the product of successive constructions, and the principal factor in this constructivism is an equilibration achieved by autoregulations that make it possible to remedy momentary incoherences, to resolve problems, and to surmount crises or periods of imbalance by a constant elaboration of fresh structures that the school can either ignore or encourage according to the methods it employs. It was therefore not a useless exercise, before examining the development of those methods, to recall some of the recent advances made by child psychology, which is now in full spate of development, though still a very long way from having opened up all of the immense territory still to be explored.

3. Development of Some Branches of Teaching

Several branches of teaching in particular have given rise since 1935 to reexaminations of their programs and of their teaching methods stimulated by three sorts of causes, sometimes overlapping and sometimes quite independent of one another. The first of these causes is the internal development of the disciplines being taught: mathematics, for example, has undergone an extremely far-reaching reorganization during the past few years, to the point where its very language has been completely transformed, and it is therefore natural that there should be an attempt to adapt students, from the very earliest age, to a new world of concepts that would otherwise remain perpetually strange to them. The second cause is the appearance of new teaching methods: the first steps in arithmetical reckoning, for example, have provided a fruitful field for the use of new physical teaching aids. The third cause is the use being made, still on a modest scale but sometimes with marked effect, of the data provided by child and adolescent psychology.

These three sorts of stimuli may of course overlap, but such is not necessarily the case, and it is therefore possible to find the most modern kind of mathematics being taught by means of the most traditional of methods, simply because no effort has been made to establish the precise relationship between newly discovered mathe-

matical structures and the operational structures spontaneously
constructed in the course of the child's mental development.

The Didactics of Mathematics

The teaching of mathematics has always presented a somewhat
paradoxical problem. There exists, in fact, a certain category of
students, otherwise quite intelligent and even capable of demon-
strating above average intelligence in other fields, who always fail,
more or less systematically, in mathematics. Yet mathematics constitutes a direct extension of logic itself, so much so that it is actually impossible to draw a firm line of demarcation between these
two fields (and this remains true whatever interpretation we give to
the relationship: identity, progressive construction, etc.). So that it
is difficult to conceive how students who are well endowed when it
comes to the elaboration and utilization of the spontaneous logico-
mathematical structures of intelligence can find themselves handi-
capped in the comprehension of a branch of teaching that bears
exclusively upon what is to be derived from such structures. Such
students do exist, however, and with them the problem.

It is usually answered in a rather facile way by talk about mathematical "aptitude" (or "bump," in memory of Gall). But, if what
we have just posited as to the relationship of this form of knowledge with the fundamental operational structures of thought is true,
then either this "aptitude" or "bump" is indistinguishable from
intelligence itself, which is not thought to be the case, or else it is
related entirely, not to mathematics as such, but to the way in
which mathematics is taught. In fact, the operational structures of
the intelligence, although they are of a logico-mathematical nature,
are not present in children's minds as conscious structures: they
are structures of actions or operations, which certainly direct the
child's reasoning but do not constitute an object of reflection on its
part (just as one can sing in tune without being obliged to construct
a theory of singing, and even without being able to read music).
The teaching of mathematics, on the other hand, specifically requires the student to reflect consciously on these structures, though
it does so by means of a technical language comprising a very par-

ticular form of symbolism, and demanding a greater or lesser degree of abstraction. So the so-called aptitude for mathematics may very well be a function of the student's comprehension of that language itself, as opposed to that of the structures it describes, or else of the speed of the abstraction process insofar as it is linked with such a symbolism rather than with reflection upon structures that are in other respects natural. Moreover, since everything is interconnected in an entirely deductive discipline, failure or lack of comprehension where any single link in the chain is concerned entails an increasing difficulty in following the succeeding links, so that the student who has failed to adapt at any point is unable to understand what follows and becomes increasingly doubtful of his ability: emotional complexes, often strengthened by those around him, then arise to complete the block that has been formed in an initiation that could have been quite different.

In a word, the central problem of mathematical teaching is that of the reciprocal adjustment between the spontaneous operational structures proper to the intelligence and the program or methods relating to the particular branches of mathematics being taught. This problem, in fact, has been profoundly modified during recent decades due to the transformations that have taken place in mathematics itself: by a process that is at first sight paradoxical, though in fact psychologically natural and clearly explicable, the most abstract and general structures of contemporary mathematics are much more closely linked to the natural operational structures of the intelligence and of thought than were the particular structures that provided the framework for classical mathematics and teaching methods.

We know, in effect, that since the research carried out by Bourbaki and his school (itself the extension of a long series of efforts in the same direction), mathematics today no longer appears as a collection of more or less separate chapters but as a vast hierarchy of interrelated structures all springing originally from a number of "mother structures" that can be combined together or differentiated in various ways. These elementary structures are three in number: the algebraic structures, characterized by a reversibility in the form of inversion $(T - T^{-1} = O)$ and whose prototype is the "group"; the ordering structures, whose reversibility is a reciprocity characteristic of systems of relationships, and whose prototype is the "network"; and the topological structures dealing with notions of continuity and proximity (bi-univocal and bi-continuous correspondences, etc.).

It so happens that these three "mother structures" correspond fairly closely with the fundamental operational structures of thought. As early as the "concrete operations" stage we have already discussed we find algebraic structures in the logical "groupings" of classes, ordering structures in the "groupings" of relationships, and topological structures in the child's spontaneous form of geometry (which is topological long before it reaches the projective forms or the metrics of Euclidean geometry, thus conforming to the theoretical order of the constitution of notions and running counter to the historical order). As soon as the stage of "propositional" operations begins we find operational structures of "groups" and "networks," etc.

Taking its inspiration from the trends initiated by Bourbaki, modern mathematics therefore emphasizes the theory of wholes and structural isomorphisms rather than traditional comparmentalizations, and an entirely new movement has become apparent, which aims at introducing such notions into our teaching at the earliest possible moment. And what is more, such a trend is fully justified, since the operations of putting together or intersecting wholes, the arrangements according to correspondences that are the sources of isomorphisms, etc., are precisely the operations constructed and utilized spontaneously by our intelligence from the age of seven or eight onward, and even more so from eleven or twelve onward (since at this stage the child can grasp the complex structure of "wholes of parts," which is the source of combinativity and "networks").

The intelligence, however, works out and employs these structures without becoming aware of them in any consciously reflective form, not in the sense that M. Jourdain spoke prose without knowing it, but rather in the sense that any adult who is not a logician nevertheless manipulates implications, disjunctions, etc., without having the slightest idea of the way in which symbolic or algebraic logic succeeds in expressing these operations in abstract and algebraic formulas. The pedagogic problem, therefore, despite the progress realized in principle by this return to the natural roots of the operational structures, still subsists in its entirety: that of finding the most adequate methods for bridging the transition between these natural but nonreflective structures to conscious reflection upon such structures and to a theoretical formulation of them.

And it is at this point, in fact, that we once more meet the conflict of which we spoke at the beginning of this section between the operational manipulation of structures and the symbolic language making it possible to express them. The most general structures of modern mathematics are at the same time the most abstract as well, whereas those same structures are never represented in the mind of the child except in the form of concrete manipulations, either physical or verbal. The mathematician who is unaccustomed to psychology, however, may suspect any physical exercise of being an obstacle to abstraction, whereas the psychologist is used to making a very careful distinction between abstraction based on objects (the source of experiment in the physical field and foreign to mathematics) and abstraction based on actions, the source of mathematical deduction and abstraction. We must avoid believing, in fact, that a sound training in abstraction and deduction presupposes a premature use of technical language and technical symbolism alone, since mathematical abstraction is of an operational nature and develops genetically through a series of unbroken stages that have their first origin in very concrete operations. Nor must we confuse the concrete either with physical experiment, which derives its knowledge from objects and not from the actions of the child itself, or with intuitive presentations (in the sense of figurative methods), since these operations are derived from actions, not from perceptual or visually recalled configurations.

These various possible misunderstandings demonstrate that, though the introduction of modern mathematics at the most elementary stages of education constitutes a great advance in principle

from the psychopedagogic point of view, the results obtained may
have been, in individual cases, either excellent or questionable
according to the methods employed. This is why the International
Conference on Public Education (International Bureau of Education and UNESCO), at its 1956 session, inserted the following articles in its Recommendation No. 43 (The Teaching of Mathematics in Secondary Schools):

20. It is important (a) to guide the student into forming his
own ideas and discovering mathematical relations and properties himself, rather than imposing ready-made adult thought
upon him; (b) to make sure that he acquires operational
processes and ideas before introducing him to formalism; (c)
not to entrust to automatism any operations that are not already assimilated.
21. It is indispensable (a) to make sure that the student first
acquires experience of mathematical entities and relations and
is only then initiated into deductive reasoning; (b) to extend
the deductive construction of mathematics progressively; (c)
to teach the student to pose problems, to establish data, to
exploit them, and to weigh the results; (d) to give preference
to the heuristic investigation of questions rather than to the
doctrinal exposition of theorems.
22. It is necessary (a) to study the mistakes made by students
and to see them as a means of understanding their mathematical thought; (b) to train students in the practice of personal checking and autocorrection; (c) to instill in students a
sense of approximation; (e) to give priority to reflection and
to reasoning, etc.

The importance of the student's personal research emphasized in
these articles is valid at all levels. At the very first stages of initiation into arithmetical calculation, the Belgian teacher Cuisenaire
introduced concrete teaching aids in the form of small sticks comprising groups of various units and known as "numbers in colors."
The principle is exactly the same as that which was used by Miles
Audemars and Lafendel at the Maison des Petits in Geneva, but

their innovation consisted in distinguishing between the sticks of various unit lengths, 1, 2, 3, etc., by their respective colors. Both the introduction of colors and the principle itself of the correspondence between spatial units and numbers can, however, give rise to extremely different interpretations and applications, despite the efforts made by C. Gattegno to introduce a kind of international supervision (of which we may all think what we like) of the "Cuisenaire method," since the Cuisenaire method does not in fact exist as a unified entity, but is rather a plurality of methods ranging from excellent to very bad (a remark that should not be taken as intended in any way to diminish the great merits of Cuisenaire himself). Though excellent when it gives rise to active manipulations and discoveries by the child itself, following the line of its spontaneous operational development, these aids may also tempt teachers to use them for demonstrations that are merely watched by the child, a process that does, of course, make comprehension easier than using more verbal or more static methods, but that runs the risk (and the risk is increased by the presence of the colors) of giving the configurations (and therefore the figurative aspects of thought: perception, imitation, and images) greater importance than the operations (and therefore than the operative aspects of thought: actions and operations). This risk becomes a reality, with all its attendant dangers, when the emphasis is placed definitively on the relationships of the colors (which is why the Maison des Petits decided to do without this ambivalent aid), and when the teacher, while under the impression that he is being faithful to the lines laid down by the active school, is in fact employing merely intuitive methods of teaching.

As a result of these difficulties, a series of research programs are at the moment being carried out, in Canada, in Great Britain, in Switzerland, and elsewhere, on the advantages and disadvantages of the various methods employed under the name Cuisenaire. One of the analytical processes being employed consists in using various operational tests of my own to compare the levels attained by comparable groups of children taught either by the usual methods or by the numbers-in-colors method. It appears that in this respect a partial advance in development can be observed in cases where the numbers-in-colors method is used in an active and operational way, and where, needless to say, the teachers are sufficiently in command of the elements of modern mathematics and the psychology of intellectual operations.

At higher levels, and up to the baccalaureate, or high-school graduation level (though beginning with the earliest steps in arithmetic and without using the numbers in colors) systematic trials are also now being made, notably at Neuchâtel under the direction of the mathematician and pedagogue L. Pauli, to ascertain whether it is possible to use as educational exercises the experimental aids that I myself used for psychological aims, the explicit aim of this work being to provide a way of teaching modern mathematical structures by methods based on the child's spontaneous operational structures. An attempt in this same direction, which is remarkable in the imagination shown in inventing new structural aids, has been made by Dienes in Australia and in the many other countries he has visited.

Fostering the Spirit of Experiment and Introducing Children to the Physical and Natural Sciences

Contemporary society has been profoundly transformed (and it is for the future to say whether it has been for better or for worse) by the work of physicists, chemists, and biologists. It nevertheless remains true to say that the elite formed by such specialists and inventors constitutes no more than a minute and heterogeneous fraction of the social body, first because their research has been very poorly understood, not only in their technical details but also in their general spirit, and secondly because present-day intellectual training and public education have turned out to be singularly ill-adapted to our new needs in the way of training and recruiting, both in the technical and in the scientific fields.

The traditional education of certain great countries has placed all the emphasis, in fact, upon the humanities and upon mathematics, as though the two predominant qualities of rational man were to be at ease with history and with formal deduction. As for practical experimentation, that was seen as a minor activity, useful for civilizations with an empirical philosophy (despite all that may have been said about the inadequacy of such a philosophy to meet the genuine conditions of scientific experimentation proper). Consequently, a sufficient experimental training was believed to have been provided as long as the student had been introduced to the results of past experiments or had been allowed to watch demonstration experiments conducted by his teacher, as though it were possible to sit in rows on a wharf and learn to swim merely by watching grown-up swimmers in the water. It is true that this form of instruction by lecture and demonstration has often been supplemented by laboratory work by the students, but the repetition of past experiments is still a long way from being the best way of exciting the spirit of invention, and even of training students in the necessity for checking or verification.

In which case, if the aim of intellectual training is to form the intelligence rather than to stock the memory, and to produce intellectual explorers rather than mere erudition, then traditional education is manifestly guilty of a grave deficiency. It is true that physics was born a good twenty centuries after mathematics, and for reasons that also explain why an experimental training is much more difficult to organize than classes in Latin or mathematics. But, as we noted in passing earlier on, the child spontaneously acquires between the ages of eleven to twelve and fourteen to fifteen all the intellectual instruments necessary for experimentation properly so-called. These instruments are of two sorts. First of all there are the tools of thought, in the form of a combinative and propositional operations, which enable the child to distinguish between implications and nonimplications, between nonexclusive disjunctions and exclusive disjunctions, between conjunctions and incompatibilities, and so forth. Secondly, there is a particular method of procedure, rendered possible by the operations just mentioned, that consists in dissociating factors according to previously stated hypotheses and in varying them experimentally, one by one, while neutralizing all the others, or in combining them in various ways.

Two elementary examples will suffice to show the difference of the spontaneous reactions in this respect between children of twelve to fifteen and those of seven to ten or eleven: (1) Having shown them a yellow liquid, one then gives them four colorless and odorless liquids $A-D$ together with a pipette E and asks them to reproduce the same yellow color: the children aged seven to ten will combine their liquids 2 by 2, then mix them all together, without success, whereas those aged ten to eleven will combine them 2 by 2, 3 by 3, and 4 by 4, working through all the possible combinations, and thereby discovering that to obtain the color a combination of three elements is necessary, while a fourth is a decolorant, and a fifth entirely neutral. (2) The children are given a set of rods of varying flexibility and asked to find the factors involved (length, thickness, shape of section, material) and to test the effective roles of those factors. Children of eleven to twelve are already able to discover these factors to some extent, but only by means of an overall, groping approach—arrangements according to serial correspondences, etc.—and in order to demonstrate the role played by length, for example, they may compare a long thin rod with a short thick one "so as to see the difference between them better." The children of thirteen to fifteen, on the other hand, begin by drawing up an inventory of the possible hypotheses, then examine each factor by studying its variations in isolation, in situations where all other things are equal. They therefore come to understand that a variation in two or more factors at the same time does not permit any conclusion to be drawn (except to prove that a combination of two or three factors is necessary to produce such and such a particular effect, as in the first experiment).

If, as he passes from the stage of concrete operations to that of propositional or hypothetico-deductive operations, the child becomes capable both of combining those hypotheses and of verifying them experimentally (many more examples of such spontaneously arrived at procedures in rational experimentation may be found in B. Inhelder and J. Piaget, *De la logique de l'enfant à la logique de l'adolescent,* Paris, P.U.F.), then it goes without saying that our schools owe it to themselves to develop and to direct such capacities in order to use them in the development of the experimental attitude of mind and of methods of teaching the physical sciences that will emphasize the importance of research and discovery instead of relying on mere repetition.

This is something that has at last begun to be apparent to educators in several countries, and in this respect one example we might quote is the United States, where this movement is very interesting to follow since the large field in that nation that is left to private enterprise makes it easier to distinguish the influences involved and the various stages of success attained, however partial those successes may be (or precisely because they are partial). One of the main currents of this movement began with the National Academy of Sciences in Washington, and with the note of warning sounded by such eminent physicists as G. Zacharias and F. Friedman at the famous Massachusetts Institute of Technology (M.I.T.), who emphasized the total discrepancy existing between the progressive spirit of science itself and the teaching of the sciences at all levels. At this point, in 1959, the Academy of Sciences organized a conference of experts at Woods Hole to which they invited a number of important American mathematicians, physicists, biologists, and psychologists, together with one scientist from overseas, in the person of my collaborator B. Inhelder. The work done at this conference has been summed up and interpreted in a very lively work by the psychologist J. Bruner (*The Process of Education,* Harvard University Press, 1961). M.I.T. went on to found a special department, entirely devoted to the teaching of the sciences and covering all its stages, in which professional physicists, unconcerned about taking precious time off from their research work, are to be found studying the development of new teaching methods along with psychologists and educators, and numerous applications have been attempted.

The impulse thus provided has led to the constitution of many work groups in the field, groups that do not limit themselves, as might so easily happen on the Continent, to organizing meetings and lectures, but have gone resolutely to work in the schools themselves, undertaking field experiments in teaching methods. And moreover, a remarkable thing in itself, one often finds professional

physicists in these research groups taking part in pedagogical inves-
tigations into the teaching of very young children in beginners'
classes. For example, R. Karplus, of the Department of Physics at
the Berkeley campus of the University of California, has developed
a set of teaching aids whose results he has studied himself, in order
to provide an introduction for very young children to the relativity
of viewpoints (by having the same phenomena described according
to the viewpoints of various observers) and to causality by interac-
tions as opposed to simple temporal series. (See *Piaget Rediscovered: A Report of the Conference on Cognitive Studies; A Curriculum Development,* edited by R. E. Ripple and V. N. Rockastle,
Cornell University Press, pp. 113–117.) Another example is Ben
Nichols, a professor of electrical engineering who has similarly organized an "Elementary Science Study Branch" within "Educational Services Incorporated," at the meetings of which, with the
collaboration of the psychologist and pedagogue E. Duckworth,
groups of children are compared according to whether they are able
or unable to achieve spontaneous experimental activities when presented with apparatus that will enable them to discover elementary
physical laws (*Piaget Rediscovered,* pp. 119–121).

It goes without saying that these field trials of "active" teaching
methods in the sphere of physics are coordinated with the efforts
being made to revolutionize the teaching of mathematics and even
of logic in action. This has been proved by J. A. Easley with regard
to the group of the four transformations (see Chapter 8), by
J. Kilpatrick (School Mathematics Study Group), by R. A. Davis
(Madison Project in Mathematics), by E. Berger (National Council of Teachers in Mathematics), and by others (Illinois Mathematics Projects, etc.) in recent conferences at Cornell University
and at Berkeley. (See *Piaget Rediscovered,* pp. 109, 128, 134,
139, 141.)

The Teaching of Philosophy

The undeniable revival that characterizes the teaching of the sciences from the primary school up to baccalaureate or high-school
graduation level, a revival from which we have quoted only one

example for the experimental disciplines, although we could have analyzed many more (in the U.S.S.R., etc.), raises a general educational problem that has been discussed in several regions: the teaching of philosophy at the secondary level. Such teaching, considered important in certain countries, such as France (where its usefulness is nevertheless often questioned) and nonexistent in others, where philosophy appears only in university curricula, is indubitably thought of in a variable way because it depends, even more than other branches of teaching, upon the aims assigned to it, and because those aims themselves, much more than with the other branches, reflect the ideology peculiar to the society in question.

If the principal aim of intellectual education is the training of the mind, then it follows automatically that philosophical reflection constitutes an essential objective both for those students one wishes to initiate particularly into mathematical deduction and experimental method and also for those who are orientated toward the humanities and the historical disciplines. But given that this is so, what form ought the introduction of these students to philosophy take in order to achieve such ends?

Whereas the changes that have occurred since 1935 in mathematics and in the experimental sciences have proved themselves to be general enough and clear enough in their direction to allow a large measure of agreement upon the pedagogical consequences to be drawn from those developments, the status of philosophy, despite the fact that it has likewise been modified quite profoundly, has been so in a much less apparent way, with the result that the philosophers themselves are very far from agreeing among themselves as to the significance of those subterranean movements.

The entire history of philosophy displays two principal tendencies that may be termed centripetal and centrifugal, the first of these being without doubt immutable and having changed no more between 1935 and 1965 than between the Classical Age and our own, whereas the second has become steadily more accentuated during these past thirty years.

Philosophy is, in the first place, and this is a constant common to all of its various systems, an attempt at coordinating values, in the widest sense, and at situating the values of knowledge within the totality of other human ends. From this point of view, the philosopher's aim is essentially to attain "wisdom," or a sort of reasoned faith, whether it be of a moral, social, or metaphysical nature. It therefore goes without saying that philosophical teaching, from this first point of view, will vary considerably from one country to another according to whether there exists a state philosophy (spiritual or materialistic, etc.), or whether, on the contrary, the state is a liberal one that desires to develop individuals with personal and varied opinions. It would be pointless here to describe these various modalities, the geographical distribution of which requires no comments, and which will be translated into equally variable teaching methods, graduating from initiation proper up to training in critical reflection.

But philosophy may also be thought of as a mode of knowledge, and it is here that we encounter the most serious divergencies and those increasingly apparent centrifugal tendencies that have become even more accentuated in the past few decades. (See Piaget, *Sagesse et illusions de la philosophie,* P.U.F., 1965.)

For some, philosophy includes a form of knowledge proper of a para- or supra-scientific nature: from the fact that vital values go beyond the frontiers of science and correspond to irreducible intuitions of value, it is concluded that there exists likewise an epistemic intuition, which provides a specific mode of knowledge that should be considered as standing in contrast to scientific knowledge.

For others—for whom history provides arguments of steadily increasing strength—philosophical reflection does certainly lead to the constitution of knowledge, but a knowledge with the property of being unable to advance except by means of a delimitation of problems and a refinement of methods, both of which are characteristic of scientific procedure itself: in other words, as soon as any body of philosophical knowledge tends to attain a certain precision, it results in the constitution of a new and particular science, which then becomes detached from the common trunk.

Leaving aside mathematics, which was still living in symbiosis with philosophy in the work of Pythagoras or Plato, logic is a striking example of such a dissociation: an offspring of the thought of Aristotle and the Stoics, conceived of as capable of generalization by Leibnitz, by the nineteenth century it was already acquiring its autonomy and particular techniques, which continued to become ever richer and more complex (with a new phase beginning in 1931 with the theorems of Goedelo) until the present, when logic is indissociable from mathematics, and the majority of philosophers are no longer able to teach it.

In the same way, psychology, too, was dissociated from philosophy during the early years of this century and, in many countries, is now taught in conjunction with biology under the aegis of the Faculty of Sciences. The International Association of Scientific Psychology, which includes in its membership the psychological associations of more than thirty countries, has persistently refused affiliation with the International Council of Philosophy and the Human Sciences in order to protect itself against speculation. Although, of course, everyone believes himself to be a psychologist, and since the coordination of values we referred to a moment ago implies a reference to the inner life, there still often appear "philosophic psychologies" that may be interesting to the moralist but have no relation at all to psychology.

Sociology also provides evidence of the same laws of evolution, though its development is not yet so far advanced because of the obstacles it presents to experiment and because statistics are not adequate for every purpose. As for the theory of knowledge, or epistemology, which presupposes at one and the same time an advanced logical development, precise psychological data, and an increasingly technical analysis of the growth of the sciences, it gives rise to ever more specialized researches, the most important of which are today carried out by the scientists concerned rather than by professional philosophers (theories of the foundation of mathematics, of microphysical experiment, etc.).

The result of this complex situation is an undeniable crisis in philosophy, and, consequently, in the teaching of it, as much at the university level as at the secondary-school level. In order to convince oneself of this, one need only observe the diversity that exists in the types of instruction offered in this branch of knowledge at the secondary-school level, and also the similar diversity in the types of training used to prepare those who are to be given the task of teaching philosophy.

The central problem is, of course, as is apparent from the preceding comments, the relationship between the philosophical and the scientific spirit: reconciliation, divorce, or various forms of compromise, such are the principal ideological or cultural tendencies that have resulted.

In the Eastern countries, the problem has been diminished in intensity by the fact that the official philosophy is that of dialectical Marxism, which claims to be scientific. Philosophy teaching at the secondary-school level is therefore quite simply an initiation into dialectical materialism, with various incursions into its scientific applications. In certain regions, such as Poland (whose school of logistics has for a long time been both flourishing and highly regarded), this is supplemented with a grounding in mathematical logic, which is sufficient to introduce the average student to problems of which, in our countries, students have no notion without special initiation courses. However, in certain Eastern countries Marxist dialectic itself may occur in two forms: one imperialist, which is maintained by the age-old ambitions of philosophers who make up a body to direct the course of the sciences, the other immanent, which is concerned with distinguishing in a much more positive fashion between the internal tendencies of all the sciences toward growth or development.

Another form of conciliation between the philosophical and the scientific spirit (though a more restrictive one, which entails undeniable dangers from the point of view of the sciences themselves, since their vitality is necessarily dependent upon their remaining indefinitely "open-ended"), is that of positivism or "logical empiricism," which first originated in the Vienna Circle and has since met with such great success in the Anglo-Saxon countries. But this movement, which has had such a strong influence on recent generations, is now beginning to decline, because of its inability (an inability common to all forms of empiricism) to maintain the essential role of the subject's activities.

In nonempiricist circles in the West, the crisis in philosophical instruction has been caused above all by the split between the scientific faculties and the faculties of letters at university level, and by the related split between the so-called literary and scientific departments in our secondary schools. It would be impossible to exaggerate the harm done by such compartmentalizations, the most evident result of which is the constitution of a sort of social caste of philosophers, who are called upon to deal directly with the total sum of reality without any personal initiation into what is meant by controlled scientific research. Whereas the great philosophers of the past all contributed in some way to the scientific movements of their time, or anticipated possible lines of research (as with the empiricists in the case of psychology, and Hegel in the case of sociology), today we are training specialists in transcendentalism who are then able to leap straight into the world of essences with an ease enormously increased by the fact that they are innocent of any form of scientific specialization, even in psychology. So that one may well ask whether we are not in the presence of a sort of sociological artifact, if we consider that the minds trained in this way are likely to go on and train succeeding generations in the literary departments of our secondary schools according to their own image, thereby perpetuating the divorce between the scientific and the philosophical spirit.

In certain places attempts have been made to remedy this dangerous situation. In Amsterdam, the logician Beth, who is unfortunately no longer with us, succeeded in separating the philosophical disciplines from the Faculty of Letters and forming them into an inter-faculty institute, with the power to grant its own degrees and doctorates, thereby reestablishing the unity of scientific research and philosophical reflection. Certain universities in Switzerland have tried to introduce a number of philosophy courses into the programs of the Faculty of Science and the Faculty of Letters simultaneously, and to guarantee similar parallel instruction in the two corresponding departments of the local secondary schools (*gymnases*). In Belgium, projects analogous to those already realized in Holland are now being studied.

The Teaching of "Classics" and the Problem of the Humanities

The literary disciplines and the humanities, unlike the branches of knowledge dealt with in the preceding sections, have given rise to few modifications in their teaching methods. The reason for this is perhaps that they are branches of learning whose content itself has varied very little, even though linguistics has made considerable advances and history has perceptibly broadened its perspectives. But the principal reason is without doubt dependent upon quite different considerations: established positions and the traditions of vested professional interest. Independently of the problem of their intrinsic educational value, to which we shall return later, it is undeniable, in effect, that the paucity of discussion on the teaching of the humanities (except among "planners," who are thinking of the future direction of public education in general) is above all a result of the fact that an appreciable number of the liberal professions are open only to those who passed final examinations (baccalaureate) that included Latin and/or Greek, and that the state, faced with such coercive situations, avoids raising questions to which it can see no solution when there are so many others requiring attention.

I have already indicated the absence of any precise method of verifying the utility of a knowledge of Latin and Greek in the case of doctors, for example, and it goes without saying that the usual arguments concerning medical terminology are somewhat fragile, since a grasp of the necessary roots and scientific terms may quite easily be acquired without having to devote six to eight years of one's life to general classical studies. In this respect—and without in the least seeking to employ deductive methods or the arguments of common sense in order to settle a question whose solution could quite easily be reached simply by amassing a sufficient number of properly controlled facts—it is interesting to note what has happened in certain countries that have undergone a change of political regime. Whereas in some countries there is no longer any obligation for doctors to know any Latin, the tradition is still observed in Poland, and since many students enter the medical faculties there without having received any instruction in that language, obligatory courses in Latin have been instituted specifically for would-be doctors, as, for example, in Warsaw. In Japan, the same obligation is left entirely to the discretion of the universities, while in India it is nonexistent.

But the real problems raised by classical studies in secondary schools are those of the aims pursued and the adequacy of the means employed. It is on these two points that several interesting debates have taken place, albeit solely on the theoretical plane.

The aims are of two sorts, one of them essential and not subject to discussion, the other marginal and a source of all kinds of questions. The principal aim is the development of the historical attitude of mind and a knowledge of those past civilizations from which our own societies have evolved. It goes without saying, in effect, that just as a knowledge of the exact and natural sciences, together with philosophical reflection, are indispensable to our knowledge of man in the universe, so there is another aspect of humanity that necessitates an equally complex but different kind of information: man's cultures and their history. It is therefore perfectly legitimate, taking into account individual aptitudes and future specializations, to look forward to the formation of a humanism whose role will be no less indispensable to the life of society than that played by the sciences and rational knowledge.

The marginal aim, upon which more emphasis is often laid, in fact, than upon the preceding one, is the training of the mind in general terms. I refer particularly to the hypothesis that an initiation into the dead languages constitutes an intellectual exercise, the benefits of which may then be transferred to other activities. It is argued, for example, that the possession of a language from which the student's own tongue developed and the ability to manipulate

its grammatical structures provide logical tools and develop a sub-
tlety of mind from which the intelligence will benefit later on regardless of the use to which it is put. Supporters of this hypothesis,
abusing a famous dictum on this subject, will even go so far as to
imply an absolute contrast between this subtle or analytic type of
mind (*esprit de finesse*) and the geometrical type of mind (*esprit
de géométrie*), as though the latter were exclusive to the sciences
and the former to the literary disciplines, whereas both, of course,
are found everywhere.

The question that is therefore being increasingly raised—particularly in Great Britain where, despite the force of tradition, the
study of dead languages has been perceptibly reduced in certain
sectors of secondary education—is whether a training in the clas-
sics does effectively attain the two aims assigned to it. It would be
futile to enter into any further discussion on the second aim. As we
have just seen, the research at present being undertaken by psychologists has not yet led to any certain conclusions. The question
of transference within the intelligence is, indeed, one of the most
difficult of all to settle statistically and experimentally, and we can
only wait until we have more decisive data before daring to pro-
nounce judgment on hypotheses or generally accepted opinions that
excite so much passion.

As for the acquisition of a humanist education and the formation
of the historical mind, our classical studies do, broadly speaking,
achieve these aims, though with one or two reservations that are
being formulated with increasing frequency today. As early as the
Entretiens sur les Humanités organized by the International Institute of Intellectual Cooperation in Budapest under the presidency
of Paul Valéry, that writer expressed approval of the present author's insistence that we should provide a more effective link between the study of ancient civilizations and the history of ideas:
why do we not put more emphasis on the fact that the Greeks,
while discovering and clarifying an unsurpassable ideal of beauty in
so many spheres, were also able to constitute a firmly based ideal
of rationality, the wellspring of all our Western sciences and phi-

losophy, whereas the Romans, though they produced great poets, were unable to crown their political and commercial activities with anything more than a juridical and military ideology? The Greek miracle is simply not intelligible, in effect, except upon condition that we have observed all its aspects, including the scientific ones, right up to its artistic and intellectual decadence in the Alexandrine period.

Where the teaching of the languages themselves is concerned, there exists a latent conflict between the grammarian's approach and that of the linguist, and there is some ground for concern over the obsolete character of certain traditional forms of "grammatical analysis" still being presented to the student as "logical," while modern linguistics, which represents such an incomparable fund of educational material, frequently remains almost totally absent from secondary-school programs. The reply to this is usually that the study of the dead languages is aimed less at the languages themselves (conveniently forgetting that it is precisely the study of the languages as such that is expected to lead to the "transferences" mentioned above, the authenticity of which has still not been established and which might well be more effective if they do exist with teaching methods better informed from the linguistic point of view) than at the thought of the authors concerned. But confronted with the sometimes disturbingly low standard displayed in final examinations involving a knowledge of the dead languages, one often wishes more time could be devoted to the subject matter than to those languages themselves. Indeed, the International Conference on Public Education, at its meeting in 1938, added to its Recommendation No. 14 (a somewhat conservative one at that) a 6th article couched in the following terms: "In order to ensure sufficient contact with the literatures (i.e., Greek and Latin), as a supplement to direct study of the original texts time should be found for reading them in translations, either of a juxtalinear nature or solely in the appropriate modern language."

As for history, it is well known how much the introduction of economic considerations has done to enrich its subject matter in recent decades, and this, too, raises new problems. To justify spending years of school life on the study of ancient civilizations simply on the grounds of their importance for modern civilization is only acceptable today if we take a much more broadly sociological view of the subject than has been prevalent in the past.

4. Development of Teaching Methods

Up to this point I have limited myself to indicating a number of transformations that have occurred since 1935 in various fields, while maintaining the traditional and serene viewpoint of the observer concerned solely with the nature of the branches of knowledge to be taught, with the students' intellectual comprehension, and with the permanent values of society. In the sections that follow, on the other hand, we shall be confronting the three principal new developments that characterize the new situations of education or teaching, and that determine all sorts of choices in an ever accelerating and also a coercive way. In consequence, the accounts of the following matters will gradually abandon the calm tone of research and adopt the more immediate and concrete accents of narrative or debate.

These three developments are: the staggering increase in the number of students, due to a much more universal opportunity of admission to the various forms of education; the almost directly related difficulty in recruiting a sufficiently well-trained teaching body; and the totality of the new needs, above all the economic, technical, and scientific needs, of the societies for whose benefit public education is organized.

These three factors already wield a large and evident influence on the choice of educational methods in general, and lead to very understandable conflicts between the traditional verbal methods, which are easier to use when the teaching personnel has not been able to acquire a sufficiently advanced training; the active methods, which become more and more necessary with the increasing desire to train more technicians and scientists; the intuitive or audio-visual methods, which some think may produce the same results as the active methods while accomplishing the task more swiftly; and programmed teaching, whose growing success is in some danger of making us forget the questions that it raises.

The Receptive Methods, or Methods of Transmission by the Teacher

It may appear somewhat nonsensical to discuss the traditional methods of oral teaching in a report whose purpose is to emphasize the new developments that have occurred since 1935. But it is a new fact that certain "progressive" countries such as the people's republics of the East claim justification for a teaching method essentially based on transmission by the teacher, or on the "lesson," now that they have perfected the method in detail by means of systematic and far-reaching psychopedagogic research. Needless to say, however, this research also provides continual evidence of the role played by interests and action in the students' understanding, so that a conflict arises between the implications arising from particular cases and the broad theory of a receptive education. It will therefore not be without interest to take a closer look at the development of such methods in the Eastern countries in this respect.

In fact, the latent conflict that I believe to be discernible springs from a duality of ideological inspirations that are perfectly compatible where the adult mind is concerned, but whose synthesis presents a problem in the educational field.

The first of these inspirations tends to present mental life as being the product of the combination of two essential factors: the biological factor and social life. The organic factor provides for the existence of the conditions for learning: the laws of primary "conditioning" (in the Pavlovian sense) and those of the second system of sign-forming, or the system of language. Social life, on the other hand, provides the totality of practical rules and bodies of knowledge arrived at collectively and passed on from one generation to the next. These biological and social factors are thus sufficient to account for mental life, and any appeal to the individual consciousness, given this point of view, is in danger of leading to a retrogressive individualism or idealism.

But then there is the second inspiration, from the same ideological source, that appears to fill what one might think looks suspiciously like a gap left by the first: this is the role of action in the transition between the biological and the social factors. This role played by action (or by *praxis*) has been abundantly emphasized by Marx, who quite rightly went so far as to consider perception itself as an "activity" of the sense organs. Moreover, this role has been invariably confirmed by Soviet psychologists, who have produced a great deal of very fine work on the subject.

From the point of view of the general methods of education, therefore, there subsists in effect a sort of duality of principles, or a dialectical conflict, according to whether one emphasizes the creative role of adult social life, which leads to a corresponding emphasis on the transmission of knowledge by the teacher, or whether one concentrates on the no less constructive role of action, which leads to placing an essential share of importance upon the activities of the student himself. In the majority of cases, in the people's republics, a synthesis is sought for in a system whereby the teacher directs the student but in a way that forces him into activity rather than merely giving "lessons" to the student. But it goes without saying, in these countries as everywhere else, that the lesson is always bound to conform to the natural tendencies of the teacher, since that is by far the easiest solution (and since everyone has not at his disposal either the necessary space or the wisdom of the Canadian school inspector who divided every class into two rooms, in order, he said, that the children should have time "to work," and that the teacher would not talk to all of them together the whole day long!). On the other hand, however, it also goes without saying that the share of importance accorded to action has led certain

Soviet educators to develop it in the direction of the research activities of the child itself, as is the case, for example, with Suhomlinsky and the Lipetsk School. These free activities are even greater in number, naturally enough, in extra-scholastic institutions, such as the "Pioneer" centers and the clubs attached to them. I have also visited certain boarding schools, in Rumania for example, where the vocational training offered was such as to give rise to research activities on the part of the students themselves, as well as to happy combinations between individual work and team work.

Active Methods

It would be quite untrue to say that any great current of change has appeared since 1935 to revolutionize our pedagogical methods in the direction of the active techniques. The main reason for this is certainly not one of principle—as we have just seen to be the case in certain Eastern countries—since with us fewer and fewer objections are now being raised on a theoretical level to a systematic exploitation of the students' own activities. A certain number of misunderstandings have also been dissipated, at least in theory, and of these the two principal ones are the following:

In the first place, it has finally been understood that an active school is not necessarily a school of manual labor, and, although the child's activity at certain levels necessarily entails the manipulation of objects and even a certain amount of actual physical groping, insofar as elementary logico-mathematical notions, for example, are derived, not from the objects manipulated, but from the actions of the child and their coordination, that at other levels the most authentic research activity may take place in the spheres of reflection, of the most advanced abstraction, and of verbal manipulations (provided they are spontaneous and not imposed on the child at the risk of remaining partially uncomprehended).

It has also been finally understood, at least on a theoretical level, that interest in no way excludes effort—quite the contrary in fact—and that an education providing a good preparation for life does not consist in replacing spontaneous efforts by dreary chores. It is recognized that although life does include a by no means negligible amount of imposed labor alongside other more freely accepted tasks, the necessary disciplines are still more efficacious when they are freely accepted than they are without such inner acceptance. So the active methods do not lead in any way to anarchic individualism, but rather, especially if they include a combination of individual work and team work, to a training in autodiscipline and voluntary effort.

However, though these views are much more widely accepted today than heretofore, no great progress has been made in putting them into practice, simply because the active methods are much more difficult to employ than our current receptive methods. In the first place, they require a much more varied and much more concentrated kind of work from the teacher, whereas giving lessons is much less tiring and corresponds to a much more natural tendency in the adult, generally, and in the adult pedagogue, in particular. Secondly, and above all, an active pedagogy presupposes a much more advanced kind of training, and without an adequate knowledge of child psychology (and also, where mathematics and physics are concerned, without a fairly good knowledge of contemporary developments in those disciplines), the teacher cannot properly understand the students' spontaneous procedures, and therefore fails to take advantage of reactions that appear to him quite insignificant and a mere waste of time. The heartbreaking difficulty in pedagogy, as indeed in medicine and in many other branches of knowledge that partake at the same time of art and science, is in fact, that the best methods are also the most difficult ones: it would be impossible to employ a Socratic method without having first acquired some of Socrates' qualities, the first of which would have to be a certain respect for intelligence in the process of development.

Although there has been no tidal wave of active methods, and though this deficiency is only too easily explained by the difficulties that have been put in the way of even the best intentions by the recent increase in the numbers of students, by the lack of teachers, and by a considerable number of other material obstacles, we ought nevertheless to take note of certain individual and important efforts, such as that made by Freinet, and of a constant tendency to revive the major preoccupations that motivate the active methods as soon as social needs have required their reappearance. We have already noted, for example, the quite widespread movement in the United States that led to an entire rethinking of elementary instruction in mathematics and physics, and which has naturally resulted in a return to "active" methods. At its 1959 session, the International Conference on Public Education voted in favor of a long recommendation (No. 49) to the appropriate minstries on "measures intended to facilitate the recruitment and training of technical and scientific personnel." And in article 34 of this recommendation we read: "In order to increase the interest shown by students in technical and scientific studies at the primary-school stage, it is advisable to employ active methods designed to develop a spirit of experiment."

As for the individual efforts of schoolteachers whose particular inventiveness or devotion to children has enabled them to find their way with their hearts to the best methods of training intelligence pure and simple (as was the case with Pestalozzi), I could quote a great number of them in the most various countries, some French-speaking, some German-speaking (considerable achievements have been made in both Germany and Austria since the defeat of Nazism), Italian-speaking, English-speaking, etc. But I shall limit myself, as an example of what can be done with modest means and without any particular encouragment from the appropriate governmental bodies, to recalling the remarkable work accomplished by Freinet, which has achieved a wide dissemination in many French-speaking areas, including French Canada. Without concerning himself overmuch with child psychology, and spurred on above all by his social preoccupations (while nevertheless keeping his distance with respect to those doctrines discussed earlier that emphasize the role of transmission by the teacher), Freinet attempted above all else to turn the school into a center for activities that are constantly in communion with those of the surrounding social collectivity. His famous idea of using printing in his school constitutes no more than one particular illustration among many in this respect, though it is an especially instructive one, since it is obvious that a child who is himself printing small fragments of text will succeed in learning to read, write, and spell in a very different manner from one who has no idea at all how the printed documents he has to use are made. Without explicitly aiming at an education of the intelligence and a method of acquiring knowledge in general through the medium of action, Freinet thus achieved these constant objectives of the active school by directing his thought above all to the development of the child's interest and his social training. And without priding himself on any theories, he thereby attained what are without doubt the two most central truths of the psychology of the cognitive functions: that the development of intellectual operations proceeds from effective action in the fullest sense (which is to say, including interests, though this in no way means that the latter are exclusively utilitarian), since logic is before all else the expression of the general coordination of actions; and secondly, that this general coordination of the actions necessarily includes a social dimension, since the inter-individual coordination of actions and their intra-individual coordination constitute a single and identical process, the individual's operations all being socialized, and cooperation in its strict sense consisting in a pooling of each individual's operations.

Intuitive Methods

One of the causes of the slowness with which the active methods have been adopted, a cause that itself springs from the insufficient psychological training of the majority of educators, is the confusion that sometimes occurs between the active methods and the intuitive methods. A certain number of pedagogues in fact—and often in the best possible faith—imagine that the latter are an equivalent of the former, or at least that they produce all the essential benefits that can be derived from the active methods.

We are faced here, moreover, with two distinct confusions. The first, which has already been mentioned, is that which leads people to think that any "activity" on the part of the student or child is a matter of physical actions, something that is true at the elementary levels but is no longer so at later stages, when a student may be totally "active," in the sense of making a personal rediscovery of the truths to be acquired, even though this activity is being directed toward interior and abstract reflection.

The second confusion consists in believing that an activity dealing with concrete objects is no more than a figurative process, in other words nothing but a way of producing a sort of precise copy, in perceptions or mental images, of the objects in question. In this way it is forgotten that knowledge is not at all the same thing as making a figurative copy of reality for oneself, but that it invariably consists in operative processes leading to a transformation of reality, either in actions or in thought, in order to grasp the mechanisms of those transformations and thus assimilate the events and the objects into systems of operations (or structures of transformations). It is also forgotten that the experience brought to bear on the objects may take two forms, one of which is logico-mathematical and consists in deriving knowledge, not from those objects themselves, but from the actions as such that modify the objects. And lastly, it is also forgotten that physical experiments in their turn, in which the knowledge is in fact abstracted from the objects themselves, consists in acting upon those objects in order to transform them, in order to dissociate and vary the factors they present, etc., and not in simply extracting a figurative copy of them.

Since all this has been forgotten, the intuitive methods come down, quite simply, to a process of providing students with speaking visual representations, either of objects or events themselves, or of the result of possible operations, but without leading to any effective realization of those operations. These methods, which are, moreover, traditional, are continually being reborn from their own ashes and do certainly constitute an advance in relation to purely verbal or formal teaching techniques. But they are totally inadequate in developing the child's operative activity, and it is only as a result of a simple confusion between the figurative and the operative aspects of thought that it has been believed possible to pay tribute to the ideal of the active methods while at the same time giving concrete form to the subject matter of education in this purely figurative guise.

Despite all this, however, the period between 1935 and 1965 has seen the reappearance of the intuitive methods in a great number of new guises, all of which, I must repeat, are all the more disturbing in that their champions usually believe in all good faith that they satisfy all the most modern requirements of child psychology. To begin with one example, I myself have received a Belgian textbook for beginners in mathematics, with a preface by a well-known educator, in which both the author and the writer of the preface refer to my own work and even do me the honor of considering it as one of the sources of their inspiration, even though in fact the manipulation of elementary logico-mathematical operations has been entirely banished from their method and its place given to figurational intuitions—often, indeed, essentially static ones.

There would be little point here in returning again to the subject of the Cuisenaire rods, since we have already seen that they are open to the most totally opposed methods of using them, some of them genuinely operative if the child is allowed to discover for himself the various operations made possible by spontaneous manipulations of the rods, but the others essentially intuitive or figurative when they are limited to external demonstrations and to explantions of the configurations laid out by the teacher.

One Swiss educator has had the notion of extracting the *maximum possible* dynamism and mobility from the intuitive methods by teaching mathematics, not with static images, but with films, whose visual continuity enables the child to watch the most striking decompositions and recompositions of figures in motion. For beginners in geometry, to give one outstanding example, this method provides the most remarkable illustrations of Pythagoras' theorem in which the relations involved acquire a visual clarity worthy of the highest praise. And yet, is this really training the child in geometrical reasoning and in operative construction in general? Bergson, who had a grudge against intelligence, compared its workings to the process of cinematography, and had he been correct in his comparison, this cinematic method of educational initiation would indeed be the last word in rational teaching methods. Unfortunately, however, Bergson missed the problem of operations and failed to understand in what way the operational transformation constitutes a genuine, continuous, and creative act: his critique of intelligence is, in fact, a critique, and a very profound one from this point of view, of visual representation, that is to say of the figurative and not of the operative aspects of thought. By the same token, a pedagogy based on the image, even when enriched by the apparent dynamism of the film, remains inadequate for the training of operational constructivism, since the intelligence cannot be reduced to the images of a film: it might much more correctly be compared, in fact, to the projector that ensures the continuity of the film's images, or better still, to a series of cybernetic mechanisms ensuring such a continuous flow of images by dint of an internal logic and of autoregulatory and autocorrecting processes.

In short, the image, the film, and all the audio-visual methods with which any pedagogy anxious to persuade itself of its modernity is perpetually bombarding us at the moment, are precious aids as long as they are thought of as accessories or spiritual crutches, and it is obvious that they represent a clear advance on purely verbal methods of instruction. But there exists a verbalism of the image just as there is a verbalism of the word, and compared with the active methods, the intuitive methods—when they forget the irreducible primacy of spontaneous activity and of personal or autonomous investigation of truth—are merely substituting this more elegant and refined form of verbalism for the traditional kind of verbalism.

It should, however, be noted—and this is something that must be entered as a debit rather than an asset to psychology in its pedagogical applications—that the intuitive methods have been able to draw sustenance from an entire psychological movement that has shown great merit in other respects: the movement known as Form or Gestalt psychology, which first arose in Germany before its subsequent proliferation elsewhere. It is therefore not a matter of chance that the intuitive methods have had their greatest development in German-speaking regions, where they are still looked upon with great esteem. The contribution of Gestalt psychology has been, in effect, after having revolutionized the problems of perception in an extremely profound and useful way, to seek in perceptible structures, or "gestalts," the prototype of all other mental structures, including the rational or logico-mathematical ones. And needless to say, if this thesis were true then it would constitute a definitive justification for the intuitive methods.

However, in the field of psychology itself the Gestalt theory has nowadays fallen from credit, mainly because its neglect of the subject's activities in favor of elementary and over-specialized physical or neurological structurations has brought it into conflict with the triumphant functionalist movements in Britain, the United States, France, and the U.S.S.R. Moreover a Gestalt is a structural whole that is at once nonadditive and irreversible, whereas the operational structural wholes (classifications, seriations, numbers, correspondences, etc.) are both reversible and strictly additive (2 and 2 make exactly 4, and not a little more or a little less as in the perceptual sphere). This necessarily implies that operations are not reducible to perceptual or visual "forms," and that, as a direct consequence, the intuitive educational methods must remain very much inferior in status to the operative, or active, methods.

Programmed Methods and Teaching Machines

In more or less close connection with the Pavlovian school of Soviet reflexology (the closeness varying according to individual cases), American psychology has evolved a certain number of theories of learning based on the stimulus-response view (or *S-R*). First Hull then Tolman developed detailed theories depending upon the effects of habit formation, then of "hierarchies of habits," the use of indices of significance, etc. And although agreement has not been reached among such authors as to the exact importance of these factors in detail, they all recognize the importance of external "reinforcements" (success and failure or various forms of sanction) and the requirements of relatively constant laws of learning with regard to repetition and length of time employed.

The most recent of the great American learning theorists, Skinner, the author of some remarkable experiments with pigeons (the favorite animal for such experimentation had until then been the white rat, which is particularly teachable but unfortunately suspected of degeneracy in its domesticated behavior), adopted a more resolutely positive attitude. Convinced of the inaccessible nature of the intermediate variables and of the excessively rudimentary state of our neurological knowledge, he decided to confine his attention to stimuli, or *inputs,* that could be varied at will and to observable responses, or *outputs,* and then to take account only of the direct relationships between them, ignoring the internal connections. This "empty box" conception of the organism, as it has been called, thus deliberately thumbs its nose at all kinds of mental life, human or animal, and confines itself solely to behavior in its most material aspects, ignoring any possible search for explanations in order to concentrate exclusively on the broad laws revealed by scrupulously detailed experimentation.

This being so, Skinner, already in possession of the laws of learning he had either personally verified or evolved, and freed of any theoretical preoccupations that might have hampered his testing of their general or practical application, observed in the first place that his experiments always worked much better when the interventions of the human experimenter were replaced by efficient mechanical apparatus. In other words, the pigeons produced much more regular reactions when dealing with "teaching machines" capable of applying the stimuli with greater precision and fewer minute variations. Skinner, a teacher by profession as well as a learning theorist, then had the brilliant idea that this observation of his would be equally valid when applied to humans, and that teaching machines, provided they were sufficiently well-programmed, would produce better results than an oral method of teaching susceptible of great variation in its application. And since the empty-box conception of the organism renders so many preliminary considerations of the internal factors of human learning unnecessary, it was sufficient to be familiar with the general laws of learning and with the subject matter of the branches of knowledge to be taught, in order to construct programs at least equal in content to the body of knowledge commonly required.

The experiment was tried and proved a total success. And it goes without saying, if we confine ourselves to the usual methods of teaching by means of verbal transmission and receptive processes, that it could not fail to succeed. The sentimental and the natural worriers have been saddened by the fact that schoolmasters can be replaced by machines. In my view, on the other hand, these machines have performed at least one great service for us, which is to demonstrate beyond all possible doubt the mechanical character of the schoolmaster's function as it is conceived by traditional teaching methods: if the ideal of that method is merely to elicit correct repetition of what has been correctly transmitted, then it goes without saying that a machine can fulfill those conditions correctly.

It has also been objected that the machine eliminates all affective factors, but this is not true, and Skinner justly claims that it is often possible to achieve a greater intensity of "motivation" (needs and interests) with machines than is found in many traditional "lessons." The question is, in fact, to establish whether the teacher's affectivity always performs a desirable function. Claparède had already expressed the opinion, in his day, that a sufficient period in a teacher's training should always be given over to practice in animal training, since when that training fails the experimenter is bound to accept that it is his own fault, whereas in the education of children failures are always attributed to the pupil. And in this respect, it should be noted, Skinner's machines provide evidence of good psychology in that they make use exclusively of positive reinforcements and dispense totally with negative sanctions or punishments.

The principle of programming (which Skinner tried out in his own psychology lessons before generalizing it to cover all branches of teaching) is, in effect, the following: the preliminary definitions having been given, the student must begin by drawing the correct conclusions from them, which means, in practice, selecting one of the two or three solutions the machine offers him. If he selects the right one (by pressing a button), the work-sequence continues, whereas if he makes a mistake the exercise is repeated. Each new item of information provided by the machine therefore leads to choices that provide evidence of the comprehension attained, with as many repetitions as prove necessary and with uninterrupted

progress in the event of constant successes. Any branch of learning
can thus be programmed in accordance with this principle, whether
it be a matter of pure reasoning or one of simple memorizing.

In practice, teaching machines conceived on these lines have had
a considerable success and have already given rise to a prosperous
industry. In a time of great increase in student population and
scarcity of teachers they are able to render undeniable services,
and, in general, save a great deal of time in comparison with traditional methods of teaching. They are used not only in schools but
also in commercial concerns where, for one reason or another, a
necessity exists for the rapid instruction of adults.

As for the intrinsic value of such a teaching method, that naturally depends upon the aims that are assigned to it in any particular
field. In cases where it is a matter of acquiring a set body of learning, as in the teaching of languages, the machine does seem to be
accepted as of undeniable service, especially as a means of saving
time. In cases where the ideal is to reinvent a sequence of reasoning, however, as in mathematics, though the machine does not exclude either comprehension or reasoning itself on the student's part,
it does channel them in an unfortunate way and excludes the possibility of initiative. It is interesting in this respect to note that at
the Woods Hole conference mentioned earlier (p. 53), at which
mathematicians and physicists were seeking for means of recasting
the teaching of the sciences, Skinner's propositions were received
with no more than limited enthusiasm, since the particular problem
facing the conference was less one of finding the means to achieve
accurate comprehension than that of encouraging the development
of inventive and inquisitive minds.

Generally speaking, since every discipline must include a certain
body of acquired facts as well as the possibility of giving rise to
numerous research activities and activities of rediscovery, it is possible to envisage a balance being struck, varying from subject to
subject, between the different parts to be played by memorizing and
free activity. In which case, it is possible that the use of teaching
machines will save time that would have been needlessly wasted by
more traditional methods and therefore augment the number of

hours available for active work. So that, particularly if the periods of active work include team work, with all that such work entails in the way of mutual incentives and checks, while the machine pre- supposes an essentially individualized kind of work, then this bal- ance would at the same time be realizing yet another necessary kind of balance: that between the collective and individual aspects of intellectual effort, both so essential to a harmonious school life.

But programmed teaching is still only in its beginnings, and it is a little too soon to make prophecies as to its future use. Like all teaching methods based on the study of one particular aspect of mental development, it may succeed from the point of view we have just examined while still proving inadequate when considered as a general teaching method. And this is a question, like all pedagogical questions, that cannot be resolved by any amount of abstract or notional discussion, but solely by accumulating the req- uisite amount of facts and controlled tests.

The curious fact, however, is that at the moment such tests are being made in the field of adult education rather than in the field of scholastic pedagogy proper, and there are at least two reasons for this. The first, which is saddening but also highly instructive, is that the effective results of a teaching method are much more closely tested and checked when it is destined for use on adults, who have no time to waste (and especially if that time is a financial consider- ation with a private commercial concern), than in the case of chil- dren, for whom time spent in study is just as precious in fact, but does not appear so in many people's eyes. The results of experi- ments with adults in this field must therefore be given close atten- tion, and examples that may be quoted in this respect are the courses in mathematics for aviators and the researches undertaken by certain army doctors, such as those at the Versailles center who are working in connection with the Institut de Psychologie of the Sorbonne.

The second reason is that the methods of programmed teaching are, in many cases, rendered valueless in advance by the fact that instead of constructing adequate programs based on the principle of progressive comprehension, those responsible for the programming often limit themselves to mere transposition into mechanically programmed terms of the contents of our current textbooks— and the worst textbooks at that! There seemed reason to hope that Skinner's method might at least have had the result of freeing us from the excessive tyranny of school textbooks, which are fairly widely recognized to be the source of many serious problems (and in recent years, according to some estimates, the total number of school textbooks published accounts for a half of the entire world's book production, and in editions larger than for any other sector!). And the fact is that quite often, in order to facilitate the task of programming, those involved simply make use of existing textbooks, naturally selecting those that lend themselves most easily to sequences of questions and answers cast in the most passive and automatic mold.

5. Quantitative Changes in Education and Educational Planning

Had I wished to present an optimistic picture of education and teaching since 1935, I should have begun with the present chapter and emphasized at the very outset the extraordinary expansion of education in recent decades. And this is certainly a most heartening development, in the sense that the increase in the total number of students has not been caused solely by the increase in population but also by measures of social justice that have made schooling available to categories of children, particularly adolescents previously underprivileged for economic reasons, by the increase in minimum school-leaving ages in many countries, and by the founding of many more vocational schools. But these positive aspects of educational development must not make us forget the problems that remain as to the efficacity of the educational means employed, and by considering matters solely from the quantitative angle we run the risk of falsifying the picture somewhat, for it is not always proved that this indefinite quantitative expansion can be equated with an educational success or victory.

It therefore seemed to me wiser to begin by emphasizing the problems that continue to confront us concerning the inadequacy of our pedagogic knowledge, our failure to relate that knowledge to the advances in psychology, the transformations within the various branches of knowledge, and the developments in teaching methods, before passing on to an examination of the more concrete questions whose solutions, whether arrived at in haste as each difficulty arose or by long consideration and systematic planning, must invariably be dependent on the set of problems mentioned above. It was therefore more in keeping with the objective approach to delay until this point any examination of the overall modifications imposed upon education by the recent changes in our societies, while always keeping in mind that these quantitative data are by no means unequivocal in their significance, and that they testify to the existence of problems rather than to that of solutions already found. If we wished to gauge the progress made by medicine, statistics telling us the number of patients being treated would not help a great deal, whereas a study of the results obtained from treatments with relation to their social extension would be much more instructive; and it is precisely this kind of control that pedagogy still lacks, which is why the progress achieved by state-controlled measures, however heartening it may be, nevertheless leaves an indefinite series of questions still open.

The recent changes in education are not solely quantitative, however, and in varying degrees of direct or loose correlation with the increases in our school population (teachers as well as pupils), reforms of educational structures on a large scale have visibly been growing. These educational reforms, either set in motion by an overall plan or preceding it in more or less disjointed stages, have resulted from the operation of a great many factors, the two principal ones being without contest the scientific and technical revolution and the general trend toward the democratization of society and education. Though it must be noted, here again, that the subsequent fate of a reform and its effective results are not solely a function of the finality that motivates it or of the adequacy of the new administrative and educational structures placed at the disposal of those ends: it is once again, and to a preponderant extent, upon the pedagogic methods employed that the results depend, and the very

best plans are bound to remain without a future if they do not
include a methodological revolution as well as a teleological one.
And this is why the preliminary questions we have been examining
up to this point concerning the development of the scientific mind
in both its aspects—logico-mathematical and experimental or even
technical—are not simply introductory questions but matters that
closely condition the effective dynamism of our reforms and long-
term planning.

Quantitative Data

The first essential fact is the tendency in all new countries to introduce or to make general the principle of compulsory schooling,
and also, in those that already possess it, to prolong it as long as
they possibly can. Thus in France, for example, the reform of January 1959 called for obligatory schooling "until the end of the sixteenth year for children of both sexes, French and foreign, who reach
the age of six after January 1, 1959." In the same year, the minimum school-leaving age was raised in the U.S.S.R., the Ukraine,
and Bielorussia from seven to eight. And present plans call for it to
be fixed at nine years in West Germany, ten years in Italy, etc.

Corresponding to this extension of compulsory schooling we
find, naturally enough, a number of measures aiming at a similar
extension in the abolition of payment for schooling and at increasing the number of educational grants to individuals. Wholly state
subsidized schooling, already common at primary-school level
(and often extended to cover school equipment and transport for
the pupils), is now becoming more prevalent at the secondary
level, and is even appearing in institutions of higher education. In
the U.S.S.R., for example, all entrance fees were abolished in 1956
for advanced classes in secondary schools, in all specialized secondary schools, and for all higher grades, so that schooling is now
entirely free in all the scholastic establishments in the country.

Leaving aside the racial discrimination that still subsists in certain places, the inequality of the sexes still remains an obstacle to
the spread of education in many countries. Even as late as 1952
the International Conference of Public Education felt it necessary

to vote in favor of a recommendation to Ministries of Education on the subject of "Educational opportunities for women," asking among other things for equality in the duration of compulsory schooling, as well as in exemption from the payment of fees, family allowances or rebates to cover the cost of studies, etc., thus enabling women to continue their studies at secondary, professional, technical, or university level. Progress has been made in this respect, but we have still not been presented with the detailed studies asked for by the conference dealing with the real state of the question and the proposed remedies.

Despite these handicaps, which are fortunately not widespread, the education rush has steadily increased in volume. In those countries that submitted reports to the International Bureau of Education, the number of pupils receiving pre-school education was increasing by from 6 to 7 percent every year between 1956 and 1959, and that of pupils receiving primary schooling from 6 to 8 percent a year on average between 1959 and 1963 (in some years reaching 11 to 12 percent). Out of 64 countries submitting quantitative data on secondary schooling, 59 showed increases and only 5 decreases: from 1959 to 1963 we find an average increase of from 10.5 to 13.7 percent per year (the fourth quartile beginning at 18.6 percent). Vocational training showed analogous increases, and students in the higher education category increased in proportions that vary from country to country between less than 7 percent (first quartile) and more than 17.6 percent (fourth quartile).

It is pointless to emphasize the fact that such increases entail a continual and corresponding increase in the Ministry of Education's budgets. Those budgets are invariably insufficient, especially in the case of higher education (hence the national centers of scientific research whose contributions supplement the allowances made to the universities), but they are growing constantly larger: in 1963 this rate of increase was proportionately inferior by 9 percent for the first quartile (out of 87 countries) and by more than 18.25 percent for the fourth quartile.

Another concrete index of this general trend is the number of new schools being built. Any valid comparison is difficult on this point, but we have the following figures by way of examples (again taken from the reports received by the International Bureau of Education): France announced that 13,915 new classrooms were opened in September 1961 for primary and secondary students, Poland built 4,221 primary classrooms in 1962, and Canada more than 8,000 in eight of its provinces.

To set against this, however, neither the recruitment nor the training of school staff provide any quantitative facts comparable to those above. We shall return later to this central problem, upon which the entire future of education ultimately depends. (See Chapter 8.)

Educational Planning

This massive quantitative increase in education is at once the reflection of the profound transformations following the end of the war in 1945, which have led to reforms in our educational structures and programs, and also the permanent cause or even the spur that has forced many governments to think through these reforms with a view to the future, in other words, to undertake long-term planning.

The necessity for wholesale reconstruction in the worst hit areas, the changes of political regime in numerous countries, the national emancipation of many others, the division of the world into political blocs, and the related trends toward political regroupings and unification, the sometimes beneficial sometimes catastrophic transformations in technology and the profound economic and sociological changes that have accompanied them, and lastly the resulting conflicts between cultural traditions and the necessity for readaptations—all these causes both together and interdependently have naturally been expressed, to varying degrees, in educational reforms. Astonishment is sometimes expressed that governments with so many urgent problems to be resolved always think first and foremost of educational reforms. But the social life of human beings is based essentially on the training of new generations by the preceding ones, in other words, on an external or educational form of transmission, not an internal or hereditary one, so that the first concern of a regime seeking to establish and maintain itself must be to concentrate on this scholastic training, in other words, upon the most direct means at its disposal, and one that in addition exercises an influence upon education within the family.

Thus we find, when comparing the number of total or partial reforms announced by various ministries of education in their annual reports for the International Education Yearbook, that the reforms carried out by 43 to 72 percent of the countries (out of 35 to 61 national units) between 1933 and 1938 fell to 28–45 percent during the war and rose to from 84 to 98 percent of the countries (out of 41 to 75) between 1946 and 1960.

But reforms are one thing—which we shall return to in Chapter 6—and long-term planning is another. As soon as the increase in school attendance is no longer simply proportional to the increase in the population as a whole, as soon as measures have been taken, either for reasons of social justice or under the pressure of economic factors, in order to prolong the period of compulsory schooling and to facilitate access in every way possible to the noncompulsory stages of education, then there is no choice but to think of the future and to cease regarding the structures that are best at the present moment as being inevitably bound to remain so at a more or less distant point in the future.

Of course, attempts have always been made to foresee the future course of events, and no government working out its school-building budget, for example, would fail to take predictions for the next few years into its calculations. But what is so strikingly new in our postwar civilizations (except in the U.S.S.R., where long-term social planning was already a feature of the regime) is that we have found ourselves with situations of such mobility, with such unforeseen and in part unforeseeable accelerations of change in so many fields, that our educational authorities, with varying timidity or boldness in each case, have come to admit the necessity for a functional adjustment of our educational structures to the needs of society that has been consciously sought for and worked out, rather than merely automatic or left to chance as in the past.

Until our day, there was, of course, a sort of accepted inventory of possible professions, and programs necessary to cover all the appropriate training courses were drawn up in vague agreement with professional bodies and trade associations. But, once done, it was imagined—in accordance with a sort of optimistic conception of social finality or a belief that the laws of supply and demand governing classical economics could be applied in all spheres—that the distribution of individuals throughout the various schools would always correspond in general to the anticipated aims, in other words, that a sort of statistical adaptation or automatic process of selection would do all that was necessary to fit the existing school structure and its human contents to all social requirements.

When the French minister Jean Berthoin exclaimed, "We are training two arts students for every three science students, whereas what we need is seven scientists to one arts student," he was in fact denouncing the inanity of such a vision of things, and his statement was made with reference, virtually and in principle, to information other than that available to the educational authorities alone. How is it known, in effect, that we need such and such a proportion of science students? If the Minister for Education makes such a statement, it is because he has been in consultation with economists, sociologists, technologists, or scientists, and because, going beyond mere questions of internal programs, he is looking at things from the point of view of implicitly existing plans, or of future trends involving society as a whole.

It is such considerations that have given rise to the trend toward long-term planning that has developed to varying degrees in a large number of countries during recent years. There is no question, naturally, of imposing their future professions upon students in answer to national needs, even though, in certain countries, the number of scholarships and places available in establishments where such and such a specialized training is given (an institute of psychology, for example) is fairly strictly determined and is in fact tantamount to planned selection. However, the real problem is that of providing for an adequate development in every kind of school, and at all levels, while also taking into account both the present and future needs of society with regard to the number and quality of those schools in each category and each subcategory, or department. Once this long-term plan has been put into effect (and it may either remain a total conception or be split up into individual stages allowing for delays in execution—5 or 10 year plans, etc.), it will then be a question of adjusting the student population to the framework provided by fairly flexible systems of guidance ("guidance phases," etc.) and sufficient scholastic mobility to ensure that individual choices and student selection will no longer depend solely on family traditions, the financial situation of parents, and outworn traditions and prejudices of all kinds, but upon each individual's aptitude and upon objective consideration of the future.

Chapter 6 will be devoted entirely to the question of structural reforms and adjustment of programs. But let us begin by recalling the general course taken by our attempts at long-term planning, a question discussed at length by the International Conference of Public Education at its 1962 session.

To be honest, though we hear the words long-term educational planning everywhere at the moment, the mere fact that the notion is fashionable has led to the usual semantic inflation, so that the term is, in fact, taken in all sorts of meanings, and in an effort not to appear out of date it is even applied to simple long-term programs that are in no way pure reform projects, or to plans for enlarging schools without any modification of educational structures. It is therefore wise not to use the phrase "long-term planning" except in relation to countries that have created a special educational planning department under their Ministry of Education (20 countries) and to those whose educational planning is subordinated to higher authorities appointed to deal with the coordination and planning of the general activities of the state (18 countries). And to these we can of course add those cases in which, without possessing permanent specialized organs of this sort, the ministries delegate the task of making reports or proposals to special commissions: this is the method employed in France, with its "Commission de l'équipement scolaire, universitaire et sportif" (Commission Le Gorgeu) given the task of reporting on educational prospects up till 1970, and bv Quebec Province with its "Commission Parent."

On the international level, UNESCO itself, in late 1964, on the initiative of M. Maheu, created an Office of Educational Planning whose director is answerable directly to the assistant director general in charge of education, and not to the two departments of school and higher education and adult education.

The people's republics naturally conceive of educational planning as being subordinated to the overall "plans" that determine the total activities of the nation as a whole. The result of this is a predominance of long-term plans, sometimes for five years, but as long as ten years in Bulgaria and twenty years in Bielorussia, Poland, the U.S.S.R., etc.

It is interesting to note that countries whose political regimes are very different often work out educational planning schemes of comparable lengths (though the 5 year plan is more general) and insist increasingly upon the necessity for coordinating them with social, economic, and technological forecasts. In this respect the collaboration between educators and economists, sociologists, technologists, and representatives of the exact and natural sciences is maintained not only throughout the planning process itself but also during their application, or, more precisely, during the process of checking the results. The lack of precise and above all of scientifically established statistics has often been noted as a serious obstacle to the success of these various planning stages, and the recommendation passed by the Conference on Public Education in 1962 contains a significant article (31) from this point of view: "It is important to do everything possible to achieve progress in techniques of qualitative and quantitative evaluation that will permit systematic verification of the results obtained, such verification being necessary to facilitate the drawing up of future plans."

It is to be hoped that these numerous studies and enquiries will lead, not only to the desired improvements in the matter of fitting the various forms of schooling to the needs of our social life, but also to progress in the direction of a scientific pedagogy, a *sine qua non* of any solution to the problems we still face, whether they concern the sociology of education or lie in the field of psychopedagogy.

As for the question of meeting social needs, the common characteristic of all the many "plans" on which the International Bureau of Education was able to obtain information when preparing for its 1962 session was that of manifesting "a very clear-cut and very general tendency to develop and perfect *technical, vocational, and scientific instruction,* whether at the secondary level of education or at the level of higher education . . . increase in the number of technical and vocational schools, enquiries with a view to revision of their programs, attention given in universities to faculties training engineers and specialists in the field of the applied sciences" (*Planning in Education,* B.I.E., UNESCO, pp. XII-XIV). So that, knowing as we do how very much dependent applied science is upon pure or "fundamental" research, and to what extent the training of researchers requires a remodeling of our traditional methods of education, it is in fact the entire problem of scientific schooling in general that has thus been raised as one of the very first order by current social planning projects.

Training of Technical and Scientific Personnel

Whereas at the outset attempts at long-term planning in education seemed necessary only in order to deal with the questions of aims and educational structures, the emphasis thus placed by the interdisciplinary collaboration of the planners upon the importance of technical and scientific training has raised, whether we like it or not, the questions of programs and of methodology itself, without which the "plans" must remain mere empty shells: any attempt to determine the number of years of study required for a given type of training is obviously meaningless unless one possesses information on the details of that training both with regard to the effective assimilation of the knowledge involved and, above all, with regard to the development of aptitudes for research, of practical or experimental adaptation, and even of invention.

In consequence, one of the longest recommendations passed by the International Conference on Public Education (and this is not by chance), concerning "measures intended to facilitate the recruitment and training of technical and scientific personnel" (1959), passes imperceptibly from questions of planning to methodological considerations. Where the former are concerned, it is worth noting that this recommendation specifically asks that the bodies to which special study of this question is entrusted, in collaboration with researchers, engineers, and qualified technicians and workers, should be of a permanent nature (article 2) so that they may keep account of the continual modifications in the situation. Moreover: "It is important that the educational structures conceived to meet the new requirements of technical and scientific training should be flexible enough to adapt themselves when necessary to the rapid development of science and technology themselves" (article 8). As for the questions of structure, the recommendation advocates in particular the creation of "more advanced specialized study courses at post-secondary and postgraduate levels, as well as the introduction of a doctorate in technology" (article 28).

As we noted earlier, where the question of methods is concerned, the recommendation emphasizes among other things the importance of active methods designed to develop an experimental attitude of mind (article 34) and also asks for "constant collaboration between schoolmasters and men of science" (article 36) in the development of pedagogic equipment—which is a fairly novel idea. For although such collaboration is quite common in the mathematical field, the wish that it should also take place in the fields of technical training and the development of experimental attitudes could lead to fairly revolutionary consequences. We have already seen, in fact, to what an extent traditional schooling, entirely centered as it is on the word and oral transmission, has neglected this aspect of intellectual training, and how far certain physicists have taken the problem to heart, to the extent of taking a personal interest in beginners' classes aimed at experimental training in primary schools. If our present essays in planning succeed in making this way of looking at things more general—and it will be taken all the more seriously to the extent that the pedagogues are backed by the authority of researchers and technicians—then they will have achieved the most decisive revolution the modern school could hope for.

Emphasis is often laid (and this is a point that the same recommendation is careful not to forget [article 40]) on the necessity for including subjects of general cultural value in the programs of technical and scientific schooling. But the opposite is also true, and an adequate amount of time should be kept in the teaching of the "arts" subjects for the development of the experimental attitude of mind, even if only in the psychological (or psychophysiological) field, though with a sufficient amount of active control to ensure comprehension of the extreme complexity of even the most apparently simple questions. An initiation into the methods of scientific control and the development of a constructive and critical mind constitute, in effect, one part of the new humanism that characterizes our developing culture, and it is this fact that is always borne in mind by those educators who are attempting, over and beyond the inevitable compartmentalizations, to preserve a certain unity in our scholastic training.

Vocational Instruction

Another extremely general manifestation of the same tendencies is that expressed in many countries by a wholesale reorganization of vocational instruction. Two complementary requirements have become apparent in this respect: on the one hand, an expansion of this form of education, so that it now includes a scholastic, theoretical, and above all practical education covering as great a number of trades as possible, and not merely those whose technical specialization has required such classroom training for a long while past; on the other hand, an internal enrichment of the programs taught, so that all those who work in skilled trades will have been provided with a broad general culture scarcely differentiated from the wide general education common to all forms of secondary education.

As an example of these two tendencies one can quote the expansion of vocational training in Poland. This training takes three principal forms: the primary vocational schools, training skilled workers and craftsmen (503,062 students in 1962–3, increase of 18.8 percent in 1963–4), and similar primary schools attached to industries (89,901 students in 1962–3, increase of 50.4 percent in

1963–4!); secondary technical and vocational schools which train workers (intermediate level; certificate of proficiency) for various sectors of the national economy (543,580 students in 1962–3, increase of 15.3 percent in 1963–4) and schools for workers already employed (evening and correspondence courses: 202,441 students in 1962–3, increase of 11.5 percent in 1963–4); and lastly, agricultural training schools (87,531 students in 1962–3, increase of 10.8 percent in 1963–4).

And the primary vocational schools cater for 199 professions or trades divided into 18 groups, the secondary ones for 203 specialized careers divided into 21 groups. "The number of professional and specialized trades related to the mechanization of labor and the automation of production show a notable increase; and it is the industries of basic importance that dominate this field: mining, metallurgy, the chemical industry, the machine industry, and electro-engineering" (Ministerial Report to the International Bureau of Education for 1963–4, p. 32).

But, this report adds, "over and above the function of preparing students for a skilled trade, the vocational school has always had as its aim, and always achieved, the complete development of the individual. With the continuing progress of socioeconomic developments, the practical application of this axiom becomes steadily more important" (p. 31). We should also add that conversely, in the Eastern countries, every high-school student, whether studying "arts" subjects or scientific ones, is increasingly expected to take a course of instruction within a selected industry, in order to acquire an initiation into the problems of technology and production.

The increase in the numbers of vocational schools in the West is equally notable. The problem of general cultural instruction is generally solved by the system of guidance phases, all the students passing through an intermediate school from which they are passed on either to the high schools or to the vocational schools: this being the general problem of structural reforms with which we now have to deal.

6. Structural Reforms: Programs and Problems of Guidance

The general expansion of education, of which the previous chapter has shown the explosive nature, is taking place both in the horizontal sense of an increase in the length of compulsory schooling and of increased opportunity of access to secondary and higher education, and also in the vertical sense of a more elaborate differentiation between the different forms of education and of an increase in the number of technical and vocational schools.

Such a situation, whether already a fact or foreseen in plans, immediately raises three problems to which solutions have, needless to say, been sought: that of cultural unity, or of a common educational foundation; that of educational mobility (directly related to social mobility in general), or of the possibility of moving from one sector into another, and therefore of eventual changes in orientation during the course of one's school life as particular aptitudes are revealed or situations clarified; and that of the methods employed to facilitate this orientation and to base it upon objective data as opposed to what are sometimes illusory estimates (whether derived from the students, from the parents, or, on occasion, from examinations).

After these major problems, which have received attention in almost every country, there remains another question, one that has

nothing minor about it except perhaps in the sense that it has been
less studied: the uninterrupted development of knowledge and
technology, and the desire to keep abreast of all these currents
without neglecting a common store of fundamental cultural training result in the majority of cases in an intolerable óverloading of
educational programs, which may in the end do harm to both the
physical and intellectual health of students and retard their training
proportionately to the extent of the wish to accelerate or perfect it.
This problem of scholastic overwork, which is sometimes a matter
of more concern to medical circles (the International Child Center,
for example) and psychologists than to the educational authorities,
is nevertheless linked to the central question of establishing whether
the school ever teaches anything useless, especially if the emphasis is placed upon the faculties of initiative and invention rather
than upon the accumulation of a body of knowledge available
in every textbook. And this problem leads us back to that of
examinations, particularly in countries where the system of competitive examinations flourishes and where those individuals who
are most gifted and of most possible use to society may waste
months or years of their life at precisely that age when the new
ideas that will direct their future careers are taking shape within
them.

Pre-School Education

The general direction of postwar reforms, with regard to the
broad problems just mentioned, is, generally speaking, to propose
an initial course of instruction common to all pupils, lasting until
the age of eleven or twelve (sometimes more), and followed by a
"guidance phase" during the course of which appropriate
specialized training is decided upon. The age of eleven to twelve is
well chosen moreover, since this is the age at which, psychologically, the child leaves behind the stage of concrete operations
(classes, relationships, numbers, etc.) and attains that of the propositional or formal operations that enable him to make hypotheses
and reason his way toward the possible: in other words, to liberate

himself from the immediate datum in the direction of interests and projects that sooner or later reveal his true aptitudes.

But at what stage do the initial course of training and schooling proper begin? In general at about the age of seven, and this age is also judiciously chosen, since it corresponds to the earliest stages in the constitution of concrete operations. But what about the period before that? And how are we to encourage the formation of those fundamental intellectual instruments?

Pre-school education (sometimes qualified with adjectives such as "nursery" or "maternal") still gives rise to modes of organization that vary a good deal from country to country, but nevertheless shows a clear-cut tendency to become increasingly widespread. In the United States, about half of all young children attend such schools; in Ontario, 1,650 public and non-state schools have at least one nursery class, and in Quebec Province the Parent Report, which is one of the most recent interesting attempts at educational planning or reform, has insisted that they should be made universal.

Though this was something that had, in fact, already been asked for by the International Conference on Public Education of 1939: "pre-scholastic education, intended for the child still below the age of compulsory school attendance, should be made the concern of educational authorities and be accessible to all children." There are, of course, economic reasons involved here, since the increasingly widespread practice of women going out to work is bound to lead to measures ensuring the care and education of young children during the hours their mothers are absent from home.

But there are psychological reasons, too, reasons whose validity is being increasingly emphasized, and it is appropriate to indicate them here, since this is one of the questions whose solution depends most upon the state of our knowledge and research in the field of child development. At a time when it was possible to consider intelligence as arising essentially from the interplay of perceptions or sensations, a "sensory education"—the model of which was provided by Froebel in his celebrated exercises—naturally seemed to answer most closely the requirements of nursery schooling. Mme Montessori later used the same principle with the addition (thanks to her power of intuition though without ever developing a theory from it) of a fair amount of action, even though it was channeled in advance by previously assembled apparatus. But today, we know that the processes of intelligence are above all matters of action and that a development of the sensorimotor functions, in the full sense of free manipulation as much as of the perceptual structuration encouraged by that manipulation, constitutes a sort of propaedeutic that is indispensable to intellectual training itself. It is doubtless true that the normal child is able to manage on its own in this respect in all situations. But by becoming familiar with the details of this development, one can encourage it to a very large extent, and this is one of the roles that pre-scholastic education is able to assume when it has sufficiently precise data upon which to rely.

It is in this spirit that the recommendation to Ministries in 1939 advocates that pre-scholastic education "should limit itself to a sensorimotor education" and that "systematic learning in the fields of reading, writing and arithmetic" should not be undertaken until primary education begins. But it clearly adds that given adequate equipment, and by making a strong enough appeal to spontaneous activity, these sensorimotor manipulations will lead to "the acquisition of numerical notions and forms." I would add that over and above these first steps in numerical and spatial intuition the activity proper to this stage also prepares the child for logical operations themselves, insofar as logic is based upon the general coordination of actions before being formulated at the level of language.

But the obstacle to the development of such pre-scholastic education—for which there is such a lively desire in many countries (France, in particular) although it is little understood in others—is naturally that the more one wishes to appeal to the spontaneous activities of small children the more psychological initiation is required. The fact is that it is much easier to deal with very young children within the framework of games or exercises entirely governed by the teacher, and the less training the latter has the less he understands how much he is losing through his lack of psychological knowledge. The same recommendation is therefore quite right in hoping (article 17) that "the training of teachers for nursery schools shall always include a specialized theoretical and practical course of instruction that will prepare them for their task. In no case should this preparation be less thorough than that of primary school staff." Hence the conclusions as to salaries and conditions of appointment that one might expect (articles 19–20).

I apologize for descending to such elementary truths in dealing with our great postwar reforms, but insofar as those reforms emphasize the necessity for developing the experimental and scientific attitude of mind, there can be no reason for neglecting what may, at first sight, appear to be the more modest conditions of that development. And those educators at "higher" levels who smile at such matters would do well to ask a question or two of those professional physicists in the United States who see nothing foolish in stooping to visit nursery schools to see if they can help to improve the methods used there.

Structural Reforms at Primary- and Secondary-School Levels·

The Langevin-Wallon project remains a model for plans of integrated reform. Presented to the Minister for National Education in 1944, it contained provision for (1) compulsory education from six to eighteen comprising three separate phases, (a) an elementary phase from six to eleven, common to all students, (b) a guidance phase (*cycle d'orientation*) from eleven to fifteen, with progressive individual specialization but possible movement from one type of instruction to another, and (c) a determinate phase from fifteen to eighteen comprising three sectors—practical, vocational, and theoretical—(2) a pre-university course (eighteen to twenty), and (3) higher education.

This project was never put into practice. It was revived with almost no changes by M. Depreux, then by Y. Delbos, and again in 1953 by A. Marie, who introduced the idea for phase 1 of two parallel courses of instruction, one "short" and the other "long." In 1955, M. Berthoin's project reduced the minimum school-leaving age to sixteen and proposed (a) a common curriculum from six to eleven (b) a guidance phase from eleven to thirteen, and (c) a phase from thirteen to sixteen with four sections: general, vocational, terminal, and higher. The Billières project in 1956 was almost identical.

On January 6, 1959, a statute (59–45) was put on the books prolonging the minimum school-leaving age to sixteen, and two decrees (59–57 and 59–58) were published providing for the reform of the baccalaureate. In 1960, the appropriate measures of application were taken and the result was the creation, at the end of the elementary phase from six to eleven, of "bridge" (*passerelles*) or "probationary" (*d'accueil*) classes ensuring the possibility of transfer from one type of education to another and guaranteeing the continuity of the student's orientation. At the end of the guidance phase, three paths are open: general, vocational, or terminal training.

This reform was naturally judged to be either excessive (the *Société des agrégés* saw it as "the death of secondary education") or insufficient (Roger Gal could see nothing in it but a compromise: "We are still waiting for a real reform.")

In August 1963 a further decree divided secondary education into two phases, the first from eleven to fifteen during which guidance is completed (beginning from the end of the first term onward) and the second from fifteen to eighteen. The first of these phases comprises parallel sections, or streams, still fairly close to one another and with the possibility of movement between them: general education stream, classical stream, modern streams (I and II according to the number of languages), and streams giving vocational training (including agricultural). The second phase provides the possibility of either a short (general or technical) education or a long one (leading to the baccalaureate in philosophy or the sciences). These multistream schools are called "colleges of secondary education."

The idea of the guidance phase has achieved acceptance and is at present being tried out in other countries, for example in the canton of Geneva, where a three-year period has been allowed for the successive organization of the three streams within the phase, all running from the ages of twelve to fifteen and providing a bridge between the present primary education and the higher secondary stage.

For purposes of comparison one can refer to the reforms in Yugoslavia, which have been introduced in stages over a period of several years after visits by experts to foreign countries and an invitation by two experts from UNESCO. Primary schooling is compulsory between the ages seven and fifteen. After that, the student moves on into either a high school or a vocational school, though with the possibility of transfer from one to the other. The high schools have two streams, one teaching languages and social sciences, the other the natural sciences and mathematics, though there are also general education classes common to all students and noncompulsory with options. The vocational training provides a flexible system of combinations between scholastic and extrascholastic training in order to insure the desired elasticity in the building up of the country's skilled labor force. University education (including all the colleges of higher education) provides for a first phase of two years' higher vocational training, a second of from four to five years corresponding to the usual university course, and a third devoted to specialized scientific research. University entrance is no longer dependent upon a baccalaurcate type of examination, but on an examination taken at the end of secondary schooling.

The Yugoslavian system is thus intended to produce an intellectual elite, while at the same time eliminating the old split between what used to be thought of as higher and lower professions, and also preserving sufficient elasticity to ensure the (horizontal) mobility of students and the necessary capacity for adaptation to any new needs that may arise in the country's economic and social life.

As will have been noted, despite ideological and terminological differences a definite conformity exists between these types of reform: the search for a "common trunk" from which differentiations can then spring, widening of the spectrum of specializations in the vocational and technical fields, and horizontal mobility between streams. These same characteristics are also found in other reform projects that have still not been put into practice, either on account of conservative opposition or because they are still too recent. Among the latter, the Parent Report in French Canada is particularly innovatory. It provides in the first place for an elementary education lasting six years, the first three of these to be devoted to learning fundamental techniques by means of the most active methods, and the second three to be taken up with initial training in methods of individual working and team work. Then comes a multistream secondary education lasting five years with the greatest possible mobility in the matter of options but with the following structural and methodological particularities:

In the first place, the elementary school should not keep pupils over the age of thirteen: the secondary school will take all children without regard to results obtained, and a preparatory year's training will be devised for the weaker students. The options available will therefore be extremely various and will include numerous technical branches, of which each student will have to choose at least one to follow throughout his secondary schooling, which implies the existence of the appropriate workshops and a regionalization of education. In the second place, the Parent Commission intends that silence and immobility shall cease to be held as the great scholastic virtues. The teaching methods will therefore be active and in strict conformity with the findings of child psychology, which in itself presupposes a more complete and more scientific training for the teachers as a whole (at the university, as we shall see, and irrespective of the level at which they will teach) and above all, the report says, a much greater degree of team work among the schoolmasters themselves!

But above all, the Parent Commission proposes the abolition of examinations, the aim of the school being the training of the student in his methods of work and not success in a final test that is based upon nothing more than an ephemeral accumulation of knowledge. The student will therefore be judged on his work, and after a two-year phase of general education followed by a three-year phase of more thorough and specialized instruction, he will receive a diploma of secondary-school study describing the results obtained.

Between this secondary education and university there is provision, lastly, for a two-year period of "pre-university and vocational" training open to all students and given in special institutes distinct from the universities themselves and extremely comprehensive in the matter of courses offered.

Methods of Guidance and the Role of School Psychologists

Over and above their obvious and invaluable usefulness from the social point of view, guidance phases also render the great pedagogic service of posing the problem of examining students in new terms.

In previous conceptions of education and educational structures each student followed a very clear-cut stream, but one chosen too early to take account of his true aptitudes or to appraise the economic or social situations in which the profession or trade for which his studies were training him would be exercised. Generally speaking, adaptation was adequate and the end of a student's studies (or the end of each phase of those studies) was crowned by success in terminal examinations devised to test a body of knowledge acquired, some of it indispensable and the rest doomed to vanish into more or less complete oblivion.

In cases of failure or momentary lack of adaptation, however, two problems remained unresolved. The first occurred when the student's education was over, regardless of the level at which the termination occurred, in the event that he either failed his final examinations or was unable, once having passed them, to find a post in the career for which he had been fitted. To ease this difficulty, career advisory offices were started, a trend that was encouraged moreover by many private and public enterprises who wished to choose their personnel on the basis of solid fact and on guarantees of relatively well-established aptitudes. These career advisory services have greatly increased in number since 1935 and have also noticeably improved their methods. University training on the part of the advisers has become increasingly common, and certain specialized establishments, such as the "Institut National d'Orientation Professionelle" founded in Paris by H. Piéron, and taken over after his retirement by M. Reuchlin, attain a high degree of scientific method, something that is not necessarily the case everywhere, however (in Switzerland, for example, the level of training of the advisers and the scientific value of the services offered differ considerably from one canton to another, and side by side with trained psychologists one also comes across other staff members who have nothing to work on other than a knowledge of the market, their mother wit, and a few tests, sometimes borrowed from psychology, sometimes not, and, in any case, quite useless without the necessary training in applying them).

In the second place, the educational structures prior to the introduction of guidance phases had no means of solving the problem of possible failures to adapt on the part of students still pursuing their studies. It was above all to remedy this state of affairs that the school psychology service was set up, since apart from the cases of clear-cut failure in which the teacher is competent to advise against a continuation of the pupil's studies or to recommend a change of school (and even in such cases it still remained to be decided if the failure was irremediable, and a thorough psychological analysis is always desirable), there also occur a great many momentary failures to adapt, either intellectual or characterial in nature, with regard to which the teacher, even if only from lack of time, may wish for the collaboration of psychologists specializing in this kind of enquiry and examination. There still remains the school doctor of course, and it may happen that a doctor-psychologist would be more useful, simply because he is competent in more fields, than a psychologist who is not a physician; but whether one is a physician or not, psychology entails a specialized, long, and thorough training, and psychology as it is practiced in the schools presupposes also, over and above basic training, a particularly delicate form of specialization.

School psychology services have therefore been set up. In France the happy idea has occurred of entrusting them to specialists qualified for the task by a twofold training: a complete training in pedagogy (diploma of education including practical courses, which among other things does away with the heterogeneity and emotional conflicts between the psychologist and the teacher) and also a no less thorough psychological training, followed by a course of specialized training.

These services have accomplished much excellent work, notably in France, where their temporary abolition in the Seine department was very badly received, and, in addition to numberless practical successes, they have provided us with some interesting scientific studies (among others, those on my own tests in relation to logico-mathematical operations). The International Conference on Public Education has interested itself in the problem, and in 1948 the ministries voted in favor of a recommendation on "the development of school psychology services." Article 3 of this recommendation defines the aims of such services as follows: recognition of backward and exceptionally gifted children, readaptation of difficult children, educational guidance and selection, pre-vocational career advice, adaptation of school programs, and checks on the results of various educational methods made in collaboration with teachers and school authorities."

It is particularly interesting to note that this recommendation does not emphasize merely those services expected in the sphere of individual or differential psychology, but also the questions of program adaptation and checks on the success of teaching methods, which come into the field of the general psychology of intellectual functions. Article 7 returns to this subject: "Scholastic psychology should not limit itself to the examination of individual cases, but should also collaborate with the teacher in analyzing the profitability of the pedagogical methods employed, and in adapting those methods to the mental development of the students."

Such was the state of the problem before guidance phases were introduced. But it goes without saying that once these latter were functioning the problems underwent radical alteration, since it is no longer primarily a question of remedying individual failures to adapt, whether momentary or final, but, on the contrary, of a continuous effort to ensure the adaptation of every student in the face of a great many possible choices or orientations.

In principle, stream selection is entrusted to the parents and the teachers. In the French system there is provision for a "guidance council," composed of all the teachers involved, which decides on the proposals to be suggested to the students. But these proposals are not imperative. If they are followed, then the student moves immediately into the stream or establishment recommended. If the choice of the parents differs from the council's recommendations, then the student has the right to present himself as a candidate for the stream or establishment the parents select but must undergo an entrance examination.

The decree of June 2, 1960 implementing the 1959 statute, makes no mention of school psychologists except at the level of the "departmental councils," which bring together representatives of the various forms of education, of the Académie, of the parents, and of the school guidance service, together with a doctor and a school psychologist, and whose task it is to implement the reforms or to suggest desirable modifications. But it need hardly be said that given the immense labor of student guidance that falls to teachers in the first terms of secondary education, the aid of the school psychologists must inevitably be sought. In Geneva, where the experiment is being undertaken on a small scale to permit a detailed analysis of individual cases, the school psychologists are being used to the full and play a necessary role in the diagnoses and, above all, in the prognoses relating to the students' aptitudes and career choices.

In this respect the guidance phases emphasize, in all its acuteness and all its universality, the important and essential problem for pedagogy, of the methods of estimating a student's intellectual value and his particular personal aptitudes. The term "intellectual value" is to be taken here in the very broadest sense, since it is obvious that thorough work habits, an inventive disposition, etc., are as much the result of character, emotional balance, and social behavior as they are of intelligence, imagination, and memory: it is not difficult, for example, to find individuals in scientific circles who possess everything needed to achieve brilliant success except self-discipline, application, ability to make choices, etc. What then are the methods that will enable us to judge and, even more important, to predict the effective work of an individual subject, and especially of a child or an adolescent?

It should be noted first of all that eleven to thirteen years is a *minimum* age for the guidance phase: it is only at that age that propositional or formal operations are beginning to become possible, and the plateau of this stage does not begin until fourteen to fifteen years, so that many spontaneous traits may not manifest themselves until later. The younger the child, in other words, the more delicate is the problem of prognosis.

The first method is long-term observation of the student's work by the teacher. The value of the judgment in this case is obviously proportional to that of the teacher: it resides in his intelligence, in his objectivity or impartiality, and especially in his capacity to dissociate permanent qualities from scholastic qualities. Much superior to the examination method, this observation of the student's work thus constitutes an essential source of information, and it is on the basis of faith in such a method that the abolition of examinations is sometimes proposed (as in the case of the Parent Commission in Canada). But two observations have often been made with regard to this matter in recent years. The first appears to be one purely of form, but nevertheless has its pedagogic importance: instead of evaluating students' work by awarding them marks given in figures (on a scale from 0 to 10 or 20, etc.), certain schools have congratulated themselves on their success in substituting verbal appraisals ("good" or "must try a little harder," etc.), which have proved themselves to be more of a spur to effort and ultimately more objective than "pass marks" whose numerical or pseudo-mathematical character is now fairly well recognized as being purely symbolic.

The other observation is more serious: the evaluation of the student's work over a certain period is not solely related to the teacher, in whom every confidence may be placed, but also to the methods employed in that work. It is only, in effect, in a school environment where active methods are employed that the student's abilities are used to the full, while in any situation governed by receptive methods the danger is that the students who are good at book learning and have an academic turn of mind will be overestimated, while other qualities unable to manifest themselves in such circumstances—and which a thorough psychological examination would reveal—will go unnoticed.

A second method of student evaluation is that of school examinations. It is being emphasized more and more what a harmful role examinations play in school work, simply because they polarize around the pursuit of ephemeral and largely artificial results the majority of the activities that ought to be concentrated upon the formation of the intelligence and good working methods. But even as indices of intellectual value, they have been the subject of severe criticism. It was in France that "docimology," or the scientific study of the true significance of examinations, was born, and H. Piéron, together with H. Laugier and many others have provided much evidence to show how variable, relatively arbitrary, and lacking in concrete significance examination marks are. Moreover, though admissible in principle as a way of estimating the comprehension achieved in a given subject, the examination cannot be limited to that function in practice, because it inevitably involves the question of memory, and a kind of memory that has no relation, generally speaking, to that which is employed consciously in life, since it is, in fact, no more than a deliberate and ephemeral accumulation—in other words, a mental artifact. The only genuine examination, given that emotional disturbances could be eliminated, would be one in which the candidate is free to use his books, notes, etc., and accomplishes a certain amount of work that is merely a continuation of what he has been doing in class: in other words, simply a part of his ordinary schoolwork, which amounts to much the same thing as the first method.

The third method of evaluation is that of regular tests, which fall into the province of scholastic psychology. It will be pointed out that these, too, are a kind of examination, but exam for exam, they do have the advantage of avoiding artificial preparation by the student, and consequently of giving much more stable results, with much more reliable and objective agreement between the various examiners. The disadvantage, however, is that these tests measure only resultants or performances without penetrating to the functional or formative mechanism behind them. In consequence, though valuable as diagnostic instruments, they are inadequate for the purpose of prognosis.

The fourth method must therefore consist of a qualificative psychological examination that will follow the functioning of the subject's thought extremely closely and reveal the operational structures that he has succeeded in mastering. This examination will therefore take the form of tests during which a set problem is resolved progressively, a procedure that will both provide suitable material for analysis and permit comparisons to be made with reference to a scale of development more ordinal in nature than metrical. It is along these lines that the Institut National d'Orientation Professionelle, at the suggestion of M. Reuchlin, has developed tests inspired by my own operational analyses, specifically for use at the pre-adolescent and adolescent levels.

Generally speaking, the services that scholastic psychology can provide seem to be increasingly valuable in proportion to their degree of reliance upon a more general and theoretically better structured psychology. Psychology has too often chased the shadow instead of the fox by searching for applications, and more particularly for measurements, before understanding the formative mechanisms and the significance of the factors measured. In this field, and analogously in many others, it may be said that there is no such thing as applied psychology but that all good psychology is susceptible of applications.

The Drawing Up of Primary- and Secondary-School Programs

The developments in the subjects to be taught (see Chapter 3) together with the continuing increase in student numbers in all sections of education and the growing mobility made possible by the guidance phases all impose frequent revisions, or recastings, of scholastic programs. This, of course, leaves us with a problem, a permanent one no doubt, but one that has also forced itself into increasing prominence during the past few years to such an extent that the International Conference of Public Education felt itself obliged to vote in favor of two recommendations, in 1958 and again in 1960, concerning "the drawing up and promulgation of programs of primary education," and then ". . . of programs of general education at secondary level." If I quote these "recommendations" so often it is not out of any exaggerated respect for an annual conference for which, it is true, I am partly responsible—but which cannot, as I shall take the opportunity of pointing out in the next chapter, in any way provide a substitute for the collective labor of specialists studying the problems scientifically; it is because, since they are the result of united efforts by official delegates from the various educational ministries, they constitute an exact reflection, not it is true of public opinion or even of the opinion of the teaching bodies involved, but certainly of the views held by the educational authorities, who possess total executive power once their proposals have been approved by their parliaments.

At all events, these recommendations (46 and 50) emphasize the dangers of overloading our school programs: "It is desirable to replace the encyclopedic contents of school programs with essential ideas" (R. 46, article 9), and: "The fairly common tendency to overload syllabuses and programs, either by introducing new material or by extending the content of each particular subject, presents a real danger; in order to counter this danger it is important that the introduction of new ideas should be compensated for by the elimination of other notions that have lost their importance . . . etc." (R. 50, article 20). A minister of education from one of the people's republics even said to me one day that, for him, the most urgent international problem in education was that of the overloading of our school curricula.

But how are we to select these "essential ideas" to which our school programs must limit themselves? The recommendations in question advocate that the drawing up and revision of the programs should be entrusted to special bodies including, of course, representatives of the teaching bodies of the levels under consideration and of the specialists in the particular subject, but also incorporating teachers from other levels and other fields—in order to provide liaisons—as well as "specialists in didactic questions," and child and adolescent psychologists.

And where secondary-school programs are concerned, the conference made detailed recommendations that "the bodies entrusted with the working out of these programs should make provision for a preliminary stage of documentation, with particular bearing on the following: (a) the characteristics and the rhythm of development in children at the age when they are affected by the crisis of adolescence; (b) the most outstanding scientific advances achieved in the various fields constituting the subjects to be taught; (c) the new data provided by didactics, both specialized and general; (d) the standard of scientific and pedagogic training of the teachers entrusted with the course; (e) the tendencies governing the cultural, social, and economic development of the modern world; (f) the comparative studies available on the programs applied in other countries; (g) the result of the experiments carried out in this respect both in this country and others" (*R*. 50 article 28).

And the conference required most emphatically that before the definitive promulgation of the programs was drawn up, they should be "subjected to carefully controlled tests, either in schools of an experimental nature or in ordinary schools . . . selected for this purpose." And by controlled tests the conference does not mean the sort of all-embracing and generalized tests that we all too often content ourselves with, but detailed researches: "Given the importance of psychological research in the drawing up and revision of secondary-school programs of teaching, it is desired that encouragement will be given to the pursuit of such research in those centers possessing the appropriate means, and that as far as is possible teachers interested in this kind of research will be associated with the projects" (*R*. 50, article 27). And in *R*. 46 article 15: "Since pedagogical research of an experimental nature is called upon to play a role of the first importance in the work of reforming and revising primary-school programs, it will be appropriate to augment the number of centers and teachers devoting themselves to such research, as well as the means put at their disposal."

Where the question of the overloading of secondary-school programs is concerned, it is of some relevance to refer to an emotional or even economic factor whose influence has sometimes been pointed out when comparing the salary structures of specialized teachers. The fact is that each of these teachers concerns himself with his particular subject for complex reasons in which intellectual fervor may be combined with questions of dignity and position within the school. It has thus occasionally become apparent that salaries calculated in exact proportion to the number of hours taught may result sooner or later in an increase in the number of those hours, whereas inclusive salaries not geared to hours taught make certain reductions in programs somewhat easier.

7. International Collaboration in Educational Matters

One of the striking features of the educational changes since the last world war is the international dimension assumed by the problems raised and the progress of international collaboration in these spheres, a collaboration that had already begun to some extent between 1925 and 1939, it is true, but which has increased immensely in its proportions between 1945 and 1965.

It is true, of course, that child psychology and pedagogy as scientific disciplines have always been international in nature, in the sense that it is impossible to pursue researches in any one country without taking account of all the other research of a similar nature being carried out in the world as a whole. The work of Dewey, Decroly, and Montessori has consequently influenced education in every country. Moreover, researchers in the educational field have naturally organized international congresses, such as the Congresses for Moral Education, which, apart from their regular meetings, and most important of all, also set up subsidiary groups with regular conferences of their own, such as the League for the New Education, headed for a long while by Mrs. Ensor, whose work has had considerable importance and is still being carried on today.

But outside of the research field, and apart from the propagandist zeal of partisans of the new methods, the educational scientists

of each country remained more or less confined within their own
national frontiers; and though, as a result of purely political influence, a smaller country might tend to follow the educational methods and structures adopted by a large one, there was little thought
given—and this is even truer of large countries than of others—to
exchanges of experimental results or to comparative studies that
might facilitate the decisions to be taken. There even existed a by
no means negligible current explicitly opposing all international
collaboration in educational matters entirely, supposedly on pre-
texts concerned with national sovereignty that seem astonishing to
us today, but, in fact, for reasons concerned above all with the
maintenance of certain traditional and philosophical positions.

Today, on the other hand, international cooperation in matters
of education has become so usual that, to give only one indication,
almost every one of the recommendations passed by the annual sessions of the Conference on Public Education includes an entire section designated, according to the individual case, by such headings
as: "International Mutual Aid," "International Collaboration,"
and "International Aspects of the Problem," whether the recommendation is concerned with financing, availability of education in
rural areas, school building, or teaching of mathematics, special
teaching for the mentally feeble, general programs, long-term planning, and so forth.

The Stages of International Collaboration in
the Field of Education

The current opposed to this collaboration was so strong when
the League of Nations was first formed that, despite the clear-cut
proposals made by Léon Bourgeois, the League decided to exclude
educational questions from its field of action.

The reaction to this deficiency was twofold. On the one hand,
the French government set up and offered to the League of Nations
in 1925 an International Institute of Intellectual Cooperation,
whose activities, though considerable, were insufficient at first to
lift the ban excluding education. On the other hand, the Institut
J. J. Rousseau, then a private institution in Geneva, succeeded in

bringing about the foundation of an International Bureau of Education, also private in character, which organized a number of congresses and modified its structure in 1929 so that it was able to include governments or education ministers as members. At the time of this reorganization, three governments took the initiative in declaring their formal membership: those of Poland, of Ecuador, and of the Republic and Canton of Geneva (the Federal Swiss government reserving its decision).

Between 1929 and 1939 the activities of the Institute of Intellectual Cooperation and those of the International Bureau of Education were oriented in complementary directions. The director general of the former, wishing to proceed by stages at his institute, which was dependent upon the League of Nations, succeeded in creating in several countries a number of "International Centers of Educational Documentation" to be coordinated by the international institute itself. The Intenational Bureau of Education, the number of whose member countries was slowly but fairly constantly growing, succeeded in organizing at its annual council meetings a presentation and discussion of general reports from the Ministries of Education represented on that council, a development that led in fact to the constitution, in 1932 and 1933, of the first two International Conferences on Public Education. The experiment having proved fruitful, a "Third International Conference on Public Education" was called in 1943, with the Swiss government acting as intermediary, and open to all member and nonmember countries of the bureau. This conference, devoted to the problems of extending the period of compulsory schooling, of admission to secondary schools, and of economies in the field of public education, was an acknowledged success, particularly in that it provided Ministers of Education with weapons that helped to safeguard them in their respective countries against the excessive economies that were at that time hitting education harder than certain other sectors. The Conferences on Public Education (at that time the phrase "the sessions of the conference" had not come into use) continued annually until 1939 then resumed in 1946.

After World War II, the same social, political, and economic causes that led to such an explosive expansion in education, as we saw earlier, rendered an extension of international collaboration not only desirable but necessary, to such an extent that no sign is now to be found of those opposing currents that had thwarted the beginnings of the movement at the time of the League of Nations. So that, under the aegis of the United Nations, there was set up the vast United Nations Educational, Scientific and Cultural Organization, or UNESCO, one of whose central activities was, of course, from the very start, that of cooperation in educational and teaching matters.

UNESCO is before all else an executive organ, and it is the only one, in the sphere with which we are now dealing, to possess the necessary financial and political means. This does not at all mean that this great organization does not undertake research, since some research is always necessary before any campaign of action, but it does not undertake research on its own behalf, except on certain points where such research is thought likely to be useful in setting some profitable trend in motion: this is particularly true, for example, in the field of the social sciences, of which UNESCO has a separate department that publishes a very lively review and contributes many examples of useful research work. On the other hand, the tasks facing us in the many spheres of education are at once so numerous and so urgent that UNESCO, as was expected of it, has concentrated its energies on a particular set of international undertakings that lie more in the field of action proper.

Everyone is aware of the organization's efforts in the struggle against illiteracy, or, as we now say, on behalf of basic education, since illiteracy is not merely a deprivation of the practices of reading and writing but a general deficiency, one involving not only the means of production and even health but also those systems of communication that are linked to the alphabet, and which serve to transmit the elementary forms of knowedge upon which the whole of life depends.

In the field of technical aid, or, as we now say, technical cooperation, UNESCO also provides continual assistance to emerging countries by sending out experts whose work contributes to the constitution, or to the functioning, of structures indispensable to the advance of education.

Quite recently, UNESCO instigated the formation of an International Institute of Educational Planning with a view to encouraging studies and exchanges of information in this essential field.

UNESCO's policy, an intelligent one, has invariably consisted in either utilizing existing bodies without absorbing them or in creating bodies for particular purposes but always allowing them intellectual, administrative, and financial autonomy (as in the case of the example just mentioned). This explains the close relationship it has developed with the International Bureau of Education and also the agreement that has led to a joint administration of the International Conference of Education by both institutions. This system has been in operation since the 1947 session and has proved satisfactory to all concerned.

The Workings and the Deficiencies of the International Conference of Public Education

A mixed committee comprising three representatives of the UNESCO Executive Council and three representatives of the International Bureau of Education decides on the questions to be placed upon the agenda of the Conference of Public Education. The offices of UNESCO then prepare this monograph, together with any particular study required concerning the questions selected, and publishes them in the form of documents which are then distributed, before becoming available to the public, to the representatives of the various ministries at that particular session of the conference. The International Bureau of Education, as its task, draws up a questionnaire on the questions selected for the agenda and sends it out to all the education ministries, the text of this questionnaire having previously been discussed and put into its final state by the institution's executive committee, on which all the member countries are represented. The results of these comparative studies are then worked up and put out as publications which, like the questionnaires, are then distributed to all the representatives at the conference before being released to the public.

The conference then meets in answer to a joint convocation by the two organizations and in accordance with lists approved by both councils. All ministries of education are in principle invited to send representatives with equal rights, whether or not they are members of the organizations issuing the invitations. But UNESCO, being one of the specialized institutions created within the United Nations, is bound by the rules that body has established. The International Bureau of Education is not attached to the United Nations, but the political wishes of majorities may also lead to certain restrictions: despite the purely technical intentions and the neutrality of those at the head of the Bureau's affairs, it has still not proved possible to invite the Chinese People's Republic, despite its 450 million inhabitants, a fact that is, of course, in complete contradiction to the spirit of the conference.

Having met, the conference then discusses the questions on the agenda and takes votes on "recommendations." It would be pointless to give further examples of these here, since I have employed quotations from them so extensively in previous chapters as expressions of the joint opinion of the 80 to 100 ministries of education customarily represented. It should be noted that these "recommendations" are, in fact, just that, and not imperative resolutions. The reason for this is, firstly, that international collaboration in matters of education can be fruitful only when carried out in a spirit of reciprocity and mutual respect such that the autonomy of each member is recognized and all interventions contrary to national sovereignty are avoided. The second reason, equally valid but of a more pedagogical nature, if that term may be employed when speaking of ministries of education, is this: imperative resolutions, if the conference were obliged to limit itself to the common denominators of those practices observed in all states, would inevitably set a rather low standard, whereas recommendations enable the most remarkable experiments and the happiest results to be given prominent positions, thus creating a spirit of emulation in achievement whose effects are far superior to any attempts at Procrustean uniformity.

This does not alter the fact, however, that in the case of certain questions directly affecting human rights and social justice—as in the fields of compulsory schooling, scholastic mobility, and the universal availability of all the branches of education, measures intended to prevent all discrimination according to race, sex, etc.—there might well be an advantage in making provision for the passing of normative measures in addition to the usual exchanges of information or mere recommendations. In these cases, the co-administrator, UNESCO, which is an executive body enjoying judicial and executive power much superior to that of the I.B.E., is perfectly designed to extend the work of the conference in this direction.

In addition to the questions that vary from year to year, at each of its sessions the Conference of Public Education then discusses the annual reports of the ministries, which are subsequently printed altogether in an *International Yearbook of Education*. These reports, which are always very instructive and useful as a means of exchanging information, lively and topical to a degree that could not even have been imagined in 1929 to 1939, indicate in particular what results have ensued from the recommendations of previous years.

The International Conference of Public Education as it is today, having been run in over twenty-seven annual sessions, certainly constitutes a useful instrument. But it would give an incomplete picture of education and teaching between 1935 and 1965 to imply that it is a wholly satisfactory one, even to those who contributed to its formation. A picture cannot be objective unless it shows the shadows as well as the highlights, and this is something I have certainly attempted to do in each of the previous chapters, starting with the very first.

To go back for a moment, then, to the very beginning of this study, it must be recognized that the educational authorities and ministries of education are one thing and educational science or research another; and indeed, this is something that the representatives of the former at the Conferences of Public Education have always recognized with great open-mindedness. But the fact nevertheless remains, when we compare this conference to others of the same kind, that it shows evidence of an imbalance of which it is not the source but from which all of contemporary education still suffers.

In the Introduction to the collected recommendations of the conference (3rd edition, 1960), I was incautious enough to speak of "a sort of international Charter or Code of Public Education, a body of pedagogical doctrine . . . etc." But let there be no misunderstanding. When the conference advocates that salaries paid to nursery-school teachers should be equal to those received by teachers in primary schools, then it is speaking the language of charters or codes and expressing an opinion different in nature, being "authorized," than that of a union congress asking for the same thing . . . or the opposite. When, on the other hand, the conference says of mathematics that it falls into the province of "the processes of logic as action" (*R.* 43, article 1), then it is within its right, but the fact is not correct because the conference has expressed it; and if the conference said the opposite then it would be in the wrong, whereas in the previous example it would still be within its rights and would still be authoritative.

In short, the ministries and their conference make the law, but they do not make scientific or pedagogical truth. Work at the international level could only be complete in this respect if the same questions, that is, those discussed by the conference, were studied either previously or subsequently by meetings of specialists in experimental pedagogy, psychology, etc., who could then present the facts at their disposal together with all their concurring or differing interpretations of them. Alternating the various questions in this way between the conference of officials and that of the experts would produce much more thorough elucidations and would lead, above all, to the drawing up of an inventory of all the questions still remaining open, the interest and urgency of which, highlighted by this kind of exchange, would provoke an increase in the amount of research done on them. Such research work is frequently asked for by the Conference of Public Education, and we must do it full justice in this respect, but a continuous and organized dialogue would nevertheless be of the very greatest service with regard to the efficacity of those requests.

It is true, of course, that the larger countries always include experts in their delegations to the Conference of Public Education (and it is precisely to those experts that we owe the best recommendations), just as the conferences of the World Health Organization are made up of representatives who are doctors as well as being delegates of their respective states. But the difference here, and it is considerable, is that in any discussion of doctrine the doctor is the representative of a science with some weight, whose authority must be acknowledged both by the ministries concerned and by the health conferences, whereas the phases of education, its methods, the training of teachers (and even down to the timetables of the lectures for that training—as if ministries of health or even of education were to decide what operations need or need not be performed in order to train a good surgeon), etc., are all organized through governmental channels.

The governments, however, depend upon parliaments and legislative bodies which, in one form or another, represent public opinion, and, consequently, that of the teaching body itself. Whereas at international level, on the other hand, the Conference of Public Education ignores such representations, except in the form of interference, which is justifiably criticized, on the part of the ministries of foreign affairs and their legal advisers! Here again, a lacuna is evident in the structure of international collaboration, and provision should be made, alongside the conferences of officials and those of the experts, for others attended by representatives of the teaching body and its unions. And in fact, such international unions or associations do exist, some of them already being represented by observers at the sessions of the official conference. There is, therefore, nothing to prevent them from taking up the same questions, studying them in a systematic manner, and making their observations known in a continuous and regular fashion. Only on that day, when a dialogue has been established with three voices representing scientific currents, the authorities, and the practitioners themselves, shall we be able to speak of anything like complete international collaboration in the educational sphere.

8. Training Teachers for Primary and Secondary Schools

There is not a single one of the questions I have touched upon in this account of education and teaching since 1935 that does not connect, sooner or later, with that of teacher training. The most admirable of reforms cannot but fall short in practice if teachers of sufficient quality are not available in sufficient quantity. Child psychology can provide us with an ever increasing fund of facts and knowledge concerning the mechanisms of development; but those facts and that knowledge will never reach the schools if the teachers have not absorbed them sufficiently to translate them into original applications. The demands of social justice and the economic needs of society may force an expansion in all sectors of education and increasing mobility for students within them; but it is still necessary that the teachers accept the very considerable responsibility of providing individual guidance, and that they acquire sufficient understanding of the complexity of these problems to provide the necessary collaboration. Generally speaking, the more we try to improve our schools, the heavier the teacher's task becomes; and the better our teaching methods, the more difficult they are to apply.

Yet, the tragic fact is that the widespread educational renaissance of recent years has coincided with an increasing dearth of teachers. And moreover, there is nothing fortuitous about this co-incidence: the same reasons that have rendered our school system inadequate have also led to the inadequacy of the social and (as an indirect consequence) of the economic position of the teacher.

These reasons may be summed up by saying that our school system, as much under left-wing as under right-wing regimes, has been constructed by conservatives (from the pedagogic point of view) who were thinking much more in terms of fitting our rising generations into the molds of traditional learning than in terms of training inventive and critical minds. From the point of view of society's present needs, it is apparent that those old molds are cracking in order to make way for broader, more flexible systems and more active methods. But from the point of view of the teachers and their social situation, those old educational conceptions, having made the teachers into mere transmitters of elementary or only slightly more than elementary general knowledge, without allowing them any opportunity for initiative and even less for research and discovery, have thereby imprisoned them in their present lowly status. And now, at the moment when we are witnessing an educational revolution of great historical importance, since it is centered on the child and the adolescent, and on precisely those qualities they possess that will be most useful to tomorrow's society, the teachers in our various schools can command neither a science of education sufficiently advanced to permit personal efforts on their part that would contribute to the further progress of that discipline, nor the solid consideration that would be attached to such a scientific, practical, and socially essential form of activity: as a consequence, the teacher's position exerts no attraction and the recruitment of teachers becomes increasingly difficult.

From every point of view then, the problem of teacher training constitutes the key problem upon whose solution those of all the other questions examined until now depend. So that the following examination of the solutions offered or proposed for this one problem, having been reserved for this final chapter, will serve as a conclusion to all the preceding analyses as a whole.

The Training of Primary-School Staff

Three sorts of systems are employed in various countries for the training of primary-school teachers: the *école normale,* or teacher training college (either residential or not), the colleges of education forming an intermediate group, and the university departments or faculties of education. The tendency over the past few years has quite clearly been toward a rise in the standard of this training, and the Conference of Public Education concluded as early as 1953 that "the training of primary-school teachers in establishments of a higher level" constitutes "an ideal we must increasingly strive to approach" (*R.* 36, article 10).

The disadvantages of the teachers' training colleges (*écoles normales*) are held to be of two kinds. The first is that they shut the primary teaching body in on itself, or in other words create a closed social entity, legitimately conscious of its merits but exposed to a sort of collective and endemic feeling of inferiority maintained by the causes given above. Everyone is aware of this phenomenon, which is a wholly artificial state of affairs created by social conditions and has become both one of the principal obstacles to recruitment (despite the improvement in salaries) and also a retarding factor in the expansion of the school system. The second disadvantage is that providing the knowledge the teachers need for the later exercise of their profession inside the training college itself ultimately results in cultural limitations, whether one wishes it or not, simply because the students are deprived of the necessary exchanges with other students studying courses leading to different professions. In particular, the psychological training so indispensable to primary-school teachers is, from this point of view, clearly more complex and difficult to impart than a secondary education, and cannot be carried out efficiently except in liaison with university research centers, where specialists can be closely observed at work. One cannot truly learn child psychology except by collaborating in new research projects and taking part in experiments, and it is useless to limit courses to exercises or practical work directed toward already known results. Such research work, however, is to be found solely in universities, and a university is the only place in which schoolteachers can learn to become researchers and to rise above the level of mere transmitters. And the same thing is equally true of experimental pedagogy itself, since its manifest destiny is to be the discipline par excellence of schoolteachers, whose individual activities would then attain a scientific status, if only they were sufficiently trained: but that training is inseparable from a high standard of psychological and sociological education.

The intermediate colleges or institutes of education attempt to remedy these defects by providing for a training in two stages: a course of general training at secondary level, acquired previously in the usual schools, and a specialized form of training given solely in these colleges or institutes. This obviously represents an advance, in that the entire emphasis can be laid in the institutes on psycho-pedagogical training. But there still remains the drawback of the future primary teachers' segregation as a social entity from secondary-school teachers, and above all from all those university students who are involved in branches of knowledge whose acquisition is inseparable from an initiation into research methods. The mere fact of having vocational training schools that are entirely divorced from the universities and solely concerned with training in the teaching of elementary subjects—whereas dentists, pharmacists, and many others, including above all the future secondary-school teachers, are required to attend a university in order to acquire their training—seems to indicate both that the vocational training of the primary-school teacher is different in status, and that it does in fact consist of nothing more than a somewhat closed-in professional training, as opposed to the initiation required for those disciplines providing opportunities for indefinite new developments and explorations. So real is this problem indeed, that in several countries a distinction is still made between "educational institutes" and "educational schools," the latter being devoted to the training of teachers of elementary classes.

In view of all this, it seems appropriate at this point to raise a question of a more general kind before going on to examine the systems of educational training in universities. By what criterion is elementary teaching judged to be easier than the teaching required in the upper classes of primary schools, and that in its turn less difficult than teaching in secondary schools? The only considera-tion that can justify this hierarchy is, of course, that of the subject matter to be taught, though solely when considered from the point of view of the standard of the knowledge itself and independently of the greater or lesser facility with which it can be assimilated by the students. So that we are immediately faced with two prelimi-nary problems to be disposed of. The first is to establish whether it is factually true that it is easier to enable a young child of seven to nine to grasp an elementary structure, say in arithmetic or lan-guage, than to enable an adolescent to assimilate a more compli-cated structure. In fact, there is nothing to prove that the second structure, though from the point of view of science or the adult himself it is effectively more complex, is in any way more difficult to communicate, if only precisely because the adolescent is closer in mental development to the thought and speech habits of the adult. The second problem is to establish, as far as the student's subsequent intellectual development is concerned, whether satisfac-tory assimilation of the structure involved (as opposed to an ap-proximate and more or less verbal assimilation) is more important at the level of higher education or at the elementary level, since success or failure in assimilating structures at the elementary stage in fact conditions the student's entire subsequent school life, whereas at the higher level there is the possibility of substitutions or autocorrection according to the student's exact level.

From this twofold point of view of the difficulties of assimilation and of the objective importance of the ideas, it is in fact permissible to hold—if one takes the psychological and even the epistemologi-cal point of view rather than that of administrative common sense —that the younger the child the more difficult it is to teach him, and the more pregnant that teaching is with future consequences. That is why one of the most interesting experiments that has been attempted in the realm of teacher training is that directed over a period of years in Edinburgh by the great psychologist Godfrey Thomson, the head of Murray House, the university's department of education: the future teachers, once they had been educated (at secondary level and then at the university) in the subject they were intending to teach, then received at Murray House a psychological and didactic training proper, and it was not until this specialized pedagogic training was finished that they selected the educational level at which they hoped to work. In other words, the future primary- and secondary-school teachers were all trained together during these final years of educational training, and without deciding from the outset which of the two categories they intended to belong to. And this produced a twofold advantage: elimination of inferiority or superiority feelings, and a training centered on the needs of the pupil rather than on the advantages of either career (both becoming equal).

Without claiming that such an ideal situation must be made universal—since the budgetary requirements for it are only too clearly of a very high order—it does at least provide an introduction to the various attempts, either already made or projected, at training primary-school teachers in universities. Moreover, it is as well in this respect not to let ourselves be blinded with words but to make quite sure in each particular case exactly what level of university education is involved. Many American "Teachers' Colleges" are nothing more in fact, from this point of view, than "educational institutes" of the intermediary type discussed earlier; open, in other words, to undergraduates who will not be required to do very much in the way of research. In other cases, however, a genuine integration of the future teacher into university life has been attempted; and this is something that is advocated, by the Parent Report in French Canada, for example, as one of tomorrow's necessary reforms.

Another experiment, carried out in Geneva during the past few years, is also instructive from the double point of view of its deficiencies and its successes. Its principle is that the future primary-school teacher should begin by acquiring his baccalaureate and then go on to spend three years receiving his specialized training. During the first of these three years, the candidates take practical courses that enable them to become acquainted with the problems, and then, in the third year, they again return to practical work. The second year, on the other hand, is spent at the university, where the candidates take courses in psychology (science faculty), pedagogy (arts faculty) and special courses at the Institut des Sciences de l'Education (Institut J. J. Rousseau), after which they take examinations for their certificate (three written and four oral exams).

The deficiencies of the system stem from the fact that the time spent at the university is undoubtedly too short to permit adequate integration. Moreover, the choice of optional subjects is an imposed one instead of being left to the individual, and the candidates are already receiving a salary, another factor that tends to set them apart from the student body as a whole. On the other hand, the initiation received is adequate to stimulate the interest of the best candidates and some of them go on later (which is to say once they have been appointed to a teaching post) to continue their studies alongside their professional activities, with the eventual possibility of acquiring diplomas or degrees in educational science or psychology, and even doctorates (the interfaculty institute being competent to confer all these).

The essential point, however, is the initiation into the psychology of mental development, and this general question goes beyond the bounds of this particular example. Everyone is in agreement (and this is true of all the systems, including the teacher training colleges –*écoles normales*) that the training of teachers necessitates a training in psychology. But the methods of the active school are still so far from being general practice in that which concerns the students themselves, that the psychological training is often reduced to no more than a set of lectures and examinations, the practical side consisting of no more than the application of a few tests. Yet it is even truer in the case of psychology than in other fields that the only way to understand the facts involved and their interpretation is to undertake some research project of one's own. This is naturally the part that is most difficult to organize, especially for beginners. In the particular example we are dealing with here the problem is solved in the following way: the institute has research programs that are planned in yearly stages by the professors and conducted by the assistants, who go every afternoon to visit premises made available in each school and question the children involved. The student teachers are associated with these research projects and accompany the assistants—in groups of two or, at the maximum, three—on these visits, so that they learn how to record facts and how to question the children, and above all so that they can make periodic reports, thus involving them with the progress of the research in periods of both failure and success. This is the kind of collaboration to which the future teachers are increasingly being invited to contribute, and it is this kind of contact with the process of gradually isolating and then collating facts that constitutes their essential training: an intellectual training, since it forces them to understand the complexity of the questions involved (whereas the lectures are concerned solely with questions already solved, and therefore apparently much simpler than they are in reality), and a moral or social training, since it gives the educator a conviction that his subject embraces indefinite opportunities for theoretical exploration and technical improvements. In a word, it is by and through research that the teacher's profession ceases to be merely a trade and even goes beyond the level of the emotional vocation to acquire the dignity of all professions that draw upon both the arts and sciences, since the sciences concerned with children and their training constitute an inexhaustible field of endeavor, now more than ever.

The Training of Secondary-School Teaching Staff

In the majority of countries secondary-school teachers are trained in universities, where they acquire *at least* one degree. They are therefore accustomed to research, at least in the subjects they will be teaching, with the result, if they are sufficiently fired with enthusiasm for those subjects in themselves, that they will be able to pick out the future researchers from among their pupils and proceed to train them with a view to such activities as well as to the assimilation of established knowledge. It often happens, however, that the more enthusiastic a secondary-school teacher is about the subject he teaches, the less interested he is in educational science as such. Or rather, pedagogy being an art as much as a science where its application is concerned, the master with a gift for teaching and creating educational contact tends to suppose that such a gift is sufficient in itself, and that a detailed knowledge of mental mechanisms is something that only primary-school teachers working with young children need, whereas at the adolescent level such psychological analyses have nothing useful to add to the classroom experience of a good teacher with an individual knowledge of his students.

One small example will serve to show what the result of such thinking may be. Modern mathematics derives in part from the theory of wholes, and one new way of teaching this subject is based nowadays on an initiation into the elementary operations involving the joining and intersection of two wholes: a reasonable enough project since the child already employs such operations spontaneously at the level of concrete operations. Yet a mathematics teacher at a secondary school was astonished at the difficulty his students displayed in manipulating such operations without errors, at the age of twelve to thirteen, when he had nevertheless furnished them with the appropriate formal definition in irreproachable terms. He was, in fact, simply forgetting the fundamental psychological difference that exists between the capacity to employ an operation spontaneously and unconsciously and the power to use reflection in order to derive an abstract formalization from it. A psychological analysis of the conditions governing the transition between these two stages of thought would have considerably simplified the problem of presentation; and simply because such an idea has not occurred to them one is constantly finding teachers today, excellent teachers otherwise, who are teaching the most advanced mathematics by means of the most antiquated educational methods.

It was therefore not without reason that the International Conference of Public Education, when dealing with the training of secondary-level teaching staff, at its 1954 session, emphasized the necessity for psychological instruction up to the same level as that bearing directly upon the subjects to be taught. In fact, however, such psychopedagogical training is much more difficult to obtain from teachers at this level than from those at the primary level, and the reasons indicated above often present an insurmountable barrier to even the best-intentioned attempts. The difficulty resides above all in the fact that if one is to understand the psychology of the adolescent mental functions it is first indispensable to have a thorough grasp of mental development in its entirety, from the earliest years up to adulthood, and that future secondary-school teachers, until they have understood how analysis of the formative processes as a whole can throw light on those peculiar to adolescence, consistently display a total lack of interest in the childhood years.

The two methods that have best succeeded up till now in persuading the trainee teachers themselves to accept such training—at least where future teachers in the sciences are concerned—are the following: the first naturally consists in associating them with psychopedagogic research bearing upon some particular logico-mathematical structure or some particular situation of physical causality; the often wholly unexpected character of the variously aged subjects is frequently sufficient to make it clear that there are problems involved of which a detailed knowledge would be of great benefit to any teacher. The second method concerns theoretical training. It often happens that future science teachers display an undisguised contempt for the psychology of development until one can succeed in making them grasp the epistemological bearing of the laws of that development. Whereas once the problems involved in the acquisition of knowledge have been posed for them in terms of relations between subject and object, or, in other words, in terms of empiricist, apriorist or constructivist interpretations, etc., they become aware of a connection with some of the central problems of their special subject and perceive the interest of research whose mere pedagogic presentation had left them unmoved.

As for future liberal-arts teachers, the state of research permits less contacts of such a kind. But with the advances in linguistic analysis bearing on the individual evolution of language, they already look promising, not only from the point of view of linguistic structuralism itself but also from that of the relations between the semiotic function and thought. Here again, the field of possible research is immense and there is no doubt that a day will come when the sciences of education, benefiting from all these contributions, will perfect techniques of immeasurably greater refinement than anything we possess today, and will succeed, by that very fact, in achieving not only a much more thorough training of the teaching body but above all its active collaboration in the perpetually self-renewing development of such disciplines.

Part II *The New Methods: Their Psychological Foundations*

How is one to define the new methods of education, and from when should we date their first appearance? To educate is to adapt the child to an adult social environment, in other words, to change the individual's psychobiological constitution in terms of the totality of the collective realities to which the community consciously attributes a certain value. There are, therefore, two terms in the relation constituted by education: on the one hand the growing individual; on the other the social, intellectual, and moral values into which the educator is charged with initiating that individual. The adult, viewing the relationship between these terms from his own point of view, began by paying attention solely to the second, and thus by conceiving of education as a mere transmission of collective social values from generation to generation. And out of ignorance, or even on account of this opposition between the state of nature characteristic of each individual and the norms of socialization, the educator concerned himself at first with the ends of education rather than with its techniques, with the finished man rather than with the child and the laws of its development.

Because of this he was led, implicitly or explicitly, to look upon the child either as a little man to be instructed, given morals, and identified as rapidly as possible with its adult models, or as the prop of various original sins, that is, as recalcitrant raw material even more in need of reclamation than of instruction. It is from this point of view that the major part of our educational methods stem. It defines the "old" or "traditional" methods of education. The new methods are those that take account of the child's own peculiar nature and make their appeal to the laws of the individual's psychological constitution and those of his development. *Passivity as against activity*.

But let there be no misunderstandings. Memory, passive obedience, imitation of the adult, and the receptive factors in general are all as natural to the child as spontaneous activity. Nor can it be said that the old methods, however antipsychological they may sometimes be, entirely neglected to observe the child in this respect. The criterion upon which a distinction between the two kinds of education is to be based should therefore be sought, not in the use made of any particular feature of the child's mentality, but in the general conception that the educator forms of the child in each case.

Is childhood a necessary evil, or have the characteristics of the childish mentality a functional significance that defines a genuine activity? According to the reply given to this fundamental question, the relation between adult society and the child to be educated will be conceived of as either unilateral or reciprocal. In the first case the child is called upon to receive from outside the already perfected products of adult knowledge and morality; the educational relationship consists of pressure on the one side and receptiveness on the other. From such a point of view even the most individual kinds of task performed by students (writing an essay, making a translation, solving a problem) partake less of the genuine activity of spontaneous and individual research than of the imposed exercise or the act of copying an external model; the student's inmost morality remains fundamentally directed toward obedience rather than autonomy. Whereas, on the other hand, to the degree in which childhood is thought of as endowed with its own genuine form of activity, and the development of mind as being included within that activity's dynamic, the relation between the subjects to be educated and society becomes reciprocal: the child no longer tends to approach the state of adulthood by receiving reason and the rules of right action ready-made, but by achieving them with his own effort and personal experience; in return, society expects more of its new generations than mere imitation: it expects enrichment.

1. The Genesis of the
New Methods

The Precursors

Though the new methods of education may thus be defined according to the genuine activity they postulate in the child and by the reciprocal character of the relation they establish between the subjects being educated and the society of which they are destined to form a part, nothing could in fact be less new than such systems. Almost all the great theoreticians in the history of pedagogy caught some glimpse of one or other of the many aspects of our present conceptions.

That the maieutics of Socrates were an appeal to the pupil's own activity rather than to his docility is something that is obvious enough, as is the fact that the reaction of Rabelais and Montaigne against the verbal education and the inhuman discipline of the sixteenth century led to some subtle psychological intuitions: the true role of interest, indispensable observation of nature, necessity for initiation into practical life, distinction between personal comprehension and memory ("To know by heart is not to know"), etc. But as Claparède has pointed out in a well-known article in the *Revue de métaphysique et de morale* (May 1912), these observations, and even those of Fénelon, Locke and others, are no more than fragmentary; in Rousseau, on the other hand, we find a total conception whose value is all the more astonishing today in that it was not inspired by any scientific experiment and that, until now, its philosophical content has too often prevented it from being judged objectively.

Because of his very convictions as to the excellence of nature and the perversion of society, Rousseau arrived, by this unexpected path, at the idea that the age of childhood does perhaps have its use, since it is natural, and that mental development is perhaps regulated by constant laws. In which case, education should make use of that mechanism instead of thwarting its progress. And from there he went on to develop an educational theory with the most elaborate refinements of detail; one that can be taken either as a brilliant anticipation of the "new methods" of education or as a mere fantasy, according as to whether one ignores Rousseau's philosophical a prioris or looks upon them, as he would wish, as inevitably linked to his sociological theories.

In fact, it is impossible when reading *Emile* to make a complete abstraction of its Rousseauist metaphysics: hence Rousseau's somewhat compromising nature as a precursor. But that observation in itself immediately makes us realize the true novelty of our own twentieth-century methods as opposed to the systems of the classical theorists. It is true that Rousseau saw that "each age has its motive force," that "the child has its own peculiar ways of seeing, of thinking, and of feeling"; it is true that he provided eloquent proof of the fact that it is impossible to learn anything other than by actively acquiring mastery of it, and that the pupil must reinvent science instead of merely repeating its verbalized formulas; it was even he who gave this piece of advice, for which much will be forgiven him: "Begin by studying your pupils, for assuredly you do not know them at all." But this continual intuition of the reality of mental development is still no more than a sociological belief, or a polemical weapon; had he personally studied the laws of this psychological maturing process whose existence he constantly postulates, he would not have dissociated the development of the individual from the social environment. The notions of the functional significance of childhood, of the phases of intellectual and moral development, of true interest and activity, are already there in his work, but they did not truly provide inspiration for the "new methods" until that moment when they were rediscovered, on the plane of objective observation and experiment, by authors more concerned with unfevered truth and systematic controls.

Among the continuators of Rousseau's work there are at least two who succeeded in realizing some of his ideas in the field of practical schooling and in this respect may be considered as the true precursors of the new methods. They are Pestalozzi, a disciple of Rousseau (1746–1827), and Froebel, a disciple of Pestalozzi (1782–1852).

Visitors to the Institut d'Yverdon are always struck by the spontaneous activity of the pupils, by the character of the teachers (older companions and trainers rather than leaders), by the experimental spirit at large in the school, where daily notes are made on the progress of the pupils' psychological development and the success or failure of the educational methods being employed. And it was thanks to this very spirit that Pestalozzi, from the very outset, was able to correct Rousseau on one capital point: a school is a true society, so that the child's sense of its responsibilities and the rules of cooperation are sufficient in themselves to provide its moral training, thereby making it quite unnecessary, in order to avoid harmful restrictions or the dangers lurking in emulation, to isolate the pupil inside his own individualism. Furthermore, the social factor has its effect in the sphere of intellectual education as well as in the moral field: like Bell and Lancaster, Pestalozzi organized a sort of mutual aid teaching system such that the children were all able to help one another with their research.

But though Pestalozzi's methods were inspired in this way, ahead of their time, by the spirit of the active school, this merely serves to make the differences between the details of his conceptions and the modern methods of the new education more glaring. What Rousseauism lacked in order to succeed in constituting a science of education was a psychology of mental development. It is true that Rousseau constantly repeated that the child is different from the adult and that each age has its own characteristics; and his belief in the constancy of the laws of psychic development was indeed so great that it even inspired him to propound his famous formula of negative education, or the uselessness of any intervention by the teacher; but what were these special characteristics of childhood and these laws of development for Rousseau? Apart from his very acute observations on the utility of exercise and exploratory gropings, and on the biological necessity of childhood, the differences he established between that state and adulthood are of an essentially negative order: the child knows nothing of reason, of a sense of duty, and so forth. Consequently, the phases of mental development he established (which some have sought to interpret as analogous to the modern theories of stages) consist quite simply in fixing, not without a certain arbitrariness, the dates at which the principal functions, or the most important manifestations, of mental life make their appearance: at such and such an age necessity, at such and such an age interest, at such and such an age reason.

In other words we find no sign of any true embryology of the intelligence or consciousness that shows how the functions are qualitatively transformed during the continuous dynamic process of their development. And, as a result, discerning the seeds of reason and moral sense in children of the very tenderest years, as everyone does, Pestalozzi (leaving aside his fruitful ideas on interest, exercise, and activity) simply reverted to the current notion of his time that the child already contains within itself the whole adult, and to the belief in mental preformation. This is why, alongside astounding achievements in the direction of the contemporary active school, the Pestalozzi institutes present so many antiquated characteristics. For example, Pestalozzi was deeply imbued with the necessity for working from the simple to the complex in all branches of teaching; but today we are all aware how very relative the notion of simplicity is to certain adult mentalities, and how the child begins by seeing life as an undifferentiated totality. Generally speaking, Pestalozzi was tainted with a certain systematic formalism, which made itself evident in his timetables, in his classification of the subjects to be taught, in his mental gymnastic exercises, and in his passion for demonstrations. His excesses in this direction demonstrate just how little account he took, in detail, of the true development of the mind.

With Froebel (1782–1852), the contrast between the idea of activity and its achievement is perhaps even greater. On the one hand there was the Rousseauist ideal of a spontaneous blossoming of the child in freedom, surrounded by things and not by books, in action and physical manipulation, and above all in a serene atmosphere without constraint or ugliness, but on the other hand, no positive notion about mental development itself. Though he intuitively understood the functional significance of play, and especially of sensorimotor exercises, Froebel believed in a sensorial phase in each individual's development: as if perception were not itself a product, and already an extremely complex one, of practical intelligence and as though the education of the senses does not need to be situated within an activation of the intelligence in its entirety. And worse still, the apparatus designed by Froebel—the famous seven series of exercises—while they did indeed represent a clear-cut advance in the direction of activity, also falsified the very idea of activity from the outset by preventing genuine creativity and by replacing concrete research, linked to the real needs of the child's life, with a kind of formalized manual labor.

The picture, generally speaking, is this: though the ideal of activity and the principles of the new methods of education may be found without difficulty in the work of the great classic educational theorists, they are nevertheless separated from us by one essential difference. Despite their intuitive or practical knowledge of childhood, they failed to establish the body of psychology necessary for the working out of educational techniques that are truly adapted to the laws of mental development. The new methods did not really come into being except with the elaboration of a true child psychology, or psychosociology; it is without doubt from the founding of such a science that we must date their existence.

But one more reservation is still necessary. During the nineteenth century, several pedagogical systems were based on psychology without falling under the head of what today are called the "new methods." There is no point in attempting a complete survey here, or in discussing the ideas of Spencer in particular; but a mention of Herbart seems indispensable. Because he provided the unfortunate model of a pedagogy drawing its inspiration from an as yet nongenetic psychology, a discussion of his work will serve to show what new material has been contributed to educational science by recent work in the field of child psychology.

Doubtless for the first time in the history of pedagogical ideas, Herbart (1776–1841) attempted in an entirely lucid and explicit way to adjust educational techniques to the laws of psychology. Everyone is aware of the wise precepts he handed down through generations of teachers and of the orderly system of practical formulas that he succeeded in codifying for the greater delight of doctrinaire minds. The entire life of the psyche consists for him of a sort of representational mechanism that eliminates intelligence as an activity—in favor of a statics and dynamics of ideas as such—and is derived in the last resort from the soul's impulse toward self-preservation; this being so, the essential problem in education is to know how to present one's subject matter so that it will be assimilated and retained: the process of apperception, which makes it possible to transform the unknown into the known, provides the key to the system. Although Herbart emphasizes the necessity for taking into account the different periods in the students' development, their individuality or above all their interest—that decisive factor in our present methods—he does so only in relation to his representational mechanics: interest is the result of apperception; the various age periods and individual types constitute its different modalities.

But did Herbart in fact transform schooling? No: there is no institution comparable to the Montessori classes, to the Decroly schools, etc., that can claim direct descent from him. Why not? Because his psychology is essentially a doctrine of the mind's receptivity and power of conservation. Herbart was unable to establish a theory of activity by reconciling the biological view of development with an analysis of the continuous construction process that is intelligence.

New Methods and Psychology

We are therefore now in a position to situate and to explain the emergence of the new methods of education representative of the contemporary era. That schooling should be adapted to the child is something everyone has constantly urged. That the child is endowed with an authentic activity of its own and that education cannot succeed without truly employing this activity and extending it is something everyone has been repeating ever since Rousseau—and indeed, that formula would have made him the Copernicus of educational science had he been able to explain precisely of what this active character of childhood consists. But to provide a positive interpretation of mental development and psychic activity was a task reserved for the psychology of this century and for the educational science that has stemmed from it.

Let there be no misunderstanding, however. Modern educational science has not emerged from child psychology in the same way that advances in industrial technique have developed, step by step, from the discoveries of the exact sciences. It is rather the general spirit of psychological research, and often, too, the very methods of observation employed, that have energized educational science in their passage from the field of pure science to that of scholastic experimentation. Though Dewey, Claparède, and Decroly, all founders of schools and inventors of exact educational techniques, are all great names in psychology, Mme Montessori, a physician, limited herself to serious anthropological and medico-psychological studies of abnormal children, allied with no more than an initiation into experimental psychology. Nor did Kerchensteiner come to psychology until his long career was at its height. But whatever the connection in the case of each of our principal innovators between child psychology and their key ideas in the field of education, there is no doubt at all that it is the great movement of modern genetic psychology that is the source of the new methods.

And in fact, contemporary psychology is differentiated from that of the nineteenth century by a radical change of viewpoint. The latter, emphasizing above all the functions of receptivity and conservation, attempted to explain the life of the mind as a whole by means of essentially static elements. In its positive form and in its attempts at scientific formulations it was mechanistic: associationism in all its aspects, and particularly in its evolutionist and genetic claims, attempted to reduce intellectual activity to combinations of inert psychic atoms (sensations and images) and to find a model for mental operations in inherently passive forms of connection (habits and associations). In its philosophical form it scarcely did any better, and limited itself to a conception of already constituted faculties in order to supplement its lack of empiricist explanations. Only Maine de Biran merits a place apart, but his lack of success and the fact that he is only really being discovered today only serve to confirm this generally unfavorable judgment.

The psychology of the twentieth century, on the other hand, was from the outset, and in all its aspects, an affirmation and an analysis of activity. There were William James, Dewey, and Baldwin in the United States, Bergson in France and Binet after *La psychologie de l'intelligence,* and Janet after *L'automatisme;* then Flournoy and Claparède in Switzerland, the Würzburg school in Germany: everywhere we find the idea that the life of the mind is a dynamic reality; intelligence, a real and constructive activity; will and personality, continuous and irreducible kinds of creativity. In short, in the field of scientific observation proper and in the reaction of experience itself against an oversimplified mechanistic view of psychology, we find a widespread effort to develop both qualitative and quantitative methods aimed at achieving a more accurate vision of that authentic process of construction that is the true development of the mind.

How the New Methods Came into Being

It was in this scientific atmosphere that the new methods of education were born. They were not the work of one isolated worker or of some pedagogue who succeeded by pure deduction in deriving a whole psychopedagogic theory of child development from some particular piece of research. They became inevitable on many fronts simultaneously.

This was because the general change in ideas about the human personality forced those with open minds to look at childhood in a different way: no longer (as was the case with Rousseau) on account of preconceived opinions on the natural goodness of man and the innocence of nature, but because of the fact, quite new in history, that science and right-minded people in general finally had at their disposal a method and a system of ideas capable of providing an account of the development of consciousness and, in particular, of the development of the infantile psyche. Only then did the true activity that all great educational innovators had dreamed of introducing into the school, and of allowing to unfold and flourish in their pupils in accordance with the internal processes of their psychic growth, become an intelligible concept and a reality susceptible of objective analysis: so that the new methods were thus effectively constituted simultaneously with child psychology and have remained closely linked with the advances of that science. This is easily demonstrated.

In the United States, the reaction against the static nature of nineteenth-century psychology made itself apparent in two ways. On the one hand the work of the pragmatists had revealed the role of action in the constitution of all mental operations, and of thought in particular; on the other, the science of mental development, or genetic psychology, had increased considerably in scope, particularly with the work of Stanley Hall and J. M. Baldwin. These two trends found their exact point of intersection in John Dewey, who in 1896 was already creating an experimental school in which the work of the students was centered upon the interests or the needs characteristic of each age group.

At the same time, in Italy, influenced above all by the anthropologist Joseph Sergi and his attempt to revolutionize educational science through the study of the child itself, Maria Montessori, having taken on the task of educating backward children, was devoting herself to an analysis of these abnormal pupils. As it became apparent to her that their afflictions were more of a psychological than of a medical order, she found herself confronted at the same time with the most central questions of intellectual development and infant education. Generalizing her discoveries with unparalleled mastery, Mme Montessori then immediately applied to normal children what she had learned from backward ones: during its earliest stages the child learns more by action than through thought; suitable school equipment, serving to provide this action with raw material, leads toward knowledge more rapidly than either the best books or even language itself. Thus the skillful observations of a psychiatric assistant on the mental mechanisms of backward children were the point of departure for a general method whose repercussions throughout the entire world have been incalculable.

And again, at the same time in Brussels, another doctor, also acquainted with psychological problems, was likewise making a study of abnormal children and similarly basing an entire educational method on his results. For it was, in effect, from the psychological analysis of the backward that Decroly derived his famous total method for the learning of reading, arithmetic, etc., and his general theory of the centers of interest and active work. Nothing could be more interesting than this synchronism in the discoveries of Dewey, Montessori, and Decroly. It shows how much the ideas of work based on interest, and of activity providing training for thought, were already latently present throughout the whole of late nineteenth-century psychology (and in biological psychology particularly).

Elsewhere, though things are more complex they are no less clear from the point of view of the influence wielded by psychological ideas. In the German-speaking countries, the active school took root very easily in a host of vocational training institutions that were already accustoming people's minds to the use of manual labor and practical research as indispensable complements to theoretical instruction. But how was the transition made from that phase, which has no direct kinship with the active school, to the decisive stage during which free activity was made the central focus of education? It is evident that manual labor has nothing inherently active about it unless it is inspired by the spontaneous research of the students themselves rather than merely by the directions of the teacher, and also that activity—in the sense of effort based on interest—can be just as reflexive and purely gnostic, even in infants, as it can be practical and manual. So that though the practice of manual work in German schools may have facilitated the discovery of the active methods it is far from explaining such a discovery.

The transition took place above all with Kerchensteiner, when, as a young science master in 1895, he devoted himself to a study of educational theory in preparation for the task of reorganizing the schools in Munich. Making use of all the work achieved by German psychology, and especially child psychology (he himself published, in 1906, the results of a vast and personally conducted inquiry into drawing which involved thousands of Bavarian school children), he arrived at his central idea: the aim of the school is to develop the student's spontaneity. This is the idea of the *Arbeitschule,* translated by P. Bovet as *l'école active,* "the active school." Moreover one has only to read Meumann, Lavy, and Mesmer to be convinced that in Germany, as everywhere else, the new methods were evolved in close connection with psychology; research into the development of the child, studies on will and thought as act, analyses of perception—the German innovators made use of all these things.

It was in Switzerland however that the famous theory of Karl Groos—that play is a preparatory exercise and therefore displays a functional significance—was given its first educational application. For it is in effect to Claparède, who had already begun in his very earliest work to react against associationism and to defend a dynamic and functional point of view, that we owe our gratitude for having understood the importance of Groos's theory for education. It was this realization that led to the teaching methods and educational games developed at the Maison des Petits in Geneva, as well as to the movement he inspired and led—both before and after the creation of the Institut J. J. Rousseau—in favor of a simultaneous study of childhood and educational techniques: *Discat a puero magister* still remains the motto of the institution he founded with P. Bovet.

It would be impossible to end this brief summary without a mention of the great importance rightly accorded in the early years of this century to the work of one of the most original of our child psychologists, Alfred Binet. Though he did not set in motion any local and typical educational movement in France itself—possibly because he never felt the desire to teach himself—his researches have had the most far-reaching repercussions, both directly and indirectly. In particular, his practical achievement in devising intelligence tests has led to innumerable research projects involving the measurement of mental development and individual aptitudes. And though the tests have not produced all the results expected of them, the problems they raised are of far greater interest than could have been foreseen at the time they first came into use: either we shall one day find good tests, or else intelligence tests will go into history as an example of a fruitful error. Apart from these tests however, Binet also rendered many other services to the new education with his theory of the intelligence and his book *Les idées modernes sur les enfants.*

2. Educational Principles and Psychological Data

To educate means to adapt the individual to the surrounding social environment. The new methods, however, seek to encourage this adaptation by making use of the impulses inherent in childhood itself, allied with the spontaneous activity that is inseparable from mental development. And they do so, moreover, with the idea that society itself will also thereby be enriched. The new education, therefore, cannot be understood in its methods and its applications unless one takes care to analyze its principles in detail and to check their psychological value on at least four points: the significance of childhood, the structure of the child's thought, the laws of development, and the mechanism of infantile social life.

The traditional school imposes his work on the student: it "makes him work." And it is doubtless true that the child is free to put a greater or lesser degree of interest and personal effort into that work, so that insofar as the teacher is a good one the collaboration that takes place between his students and himself will leave an appreciable margin for genuine activity. But in the logic of the system the student's intellectual and moral activity remains heteronomous because it is inseparable from a continual constraint exercised by the teacher, even though that constraint may remain unperceived by the student or be accepted by him of his own free will.

The new school, on the contrary, appeals to real activity, to spontaneous work based upon personal need and interest. This does not mean, as Claparède so succinctly put it, that active education requires that children should do anything they want; "it requires above all that they should will what they do; that they should act, not that they should be acted upon." (*L'éducation fonctionnelle*, p. 252). Need, the interest that is a resultant of need, "that is the factor that will make a reaction into an authentic act" (p. 195). The law of interest is thus "the sole pivot around which the whole system should turn" (p. 197).

Such a conception implies, however, a very precise notion of the significance of childhood and its activities. For to repeat with Dewey and Claparède that compulsory work is an antipsychological anomaly and that all fruitful activity presupposes an interest, means the risk of appearing to be merely restating what all the great classical educators have already affirmed so often; on the other hand, by endowing the child with the possibility of a durable kind of personal work one is postulating precisely what one is required to prove. Is childhood capable of this activity, characteristic of the highest forms of adult behavior: diligent and continuous research, springing from a spontaneous need?—that is the central problem of the new education.

A decisive observation made by Claparède will help in throwing some light on the discussion of this point. If we make a distinction between the structure of thought and psychic operations on the one hand (in other words, everything that corresponds, from the psychological point of view, to the organs and the anatomy of the organism), and their functioning on the other hand (in other words all that corresponds with the functional relationships studied by physiology), then we may say that traditional pedagogy attributed to the child a mental structure identical with that of the adult, but a different mode of functioning: "It liked to think of the child . . . as capable, for example, of grasping anything that is logically evident, or of understanding the deep significance of certain moral rules; but, at the same time, it also considered the child as functionally different from the adult, in the sense that whereas the hand is capable of laboring without a motive, of acquiring the most disparate forms of knowledge to order, of doing any work you like, simply because the school requires it, but without that work answering to any need arising within its child's self, within its child's life" (*L'éducation fonctionnelle*, p. 246–247).

In fact, it is the contrary that is true. The intellectual and moral structures of the child are not the same as ours; and consequently the new methods of education make every effort to present the subject matter to be taught in forms assimilable to children of different ages in accordance with their mental structure and the various stages of their development. But with regard to mental functioning, the child is in fact identical with the adult; like the adult, he is an active being whose action, controlled by the law of interest or need, is incapable of working at full stretch if no appeal is made to the autonomous motive forces of that activity. Just as the tadpole already breathes, though with different organs from those of the frog, so the child acts like the adult, but employing a mentality whose structure varies according to the stages of its development.

What is childhood then? And how are we to adjust our educational techniques to beings at once so like and yet so unlike us? Childhood, for the theorists of the new school, is not a necessary evil: it is a biologically useful phase whose significance is that of a progressive adaptation to a physical and social environment.

Moreover, this adaptation is a state of balance—an equilibrium whose achievement occupies the whole of childhood and adolescence and defines the structuration proper to those periods of existence—between two inseparable mechanisms: assimilation and accommodation. We say, for example, that an organism is well-adapted when it can simultaneously preserve its structure by assimilating into it nourishment drawn from the external environment and also accommodate that structure to the various particularities of that environment: biological adaptation is thus a state of balance between an assimilation of the environment to the organism and an accommodation of the organism to the environment. Similarly, it is possible to say that thought is well adapted to a particular reality when it has been successful in assimilating that reality into its own framework while also accommodating that framework to the new circumstances presented by the reality. Intellectual adaptation is thus a process of achieving a state of balance between the assimilation of experience into the deductive structures and the accommodation of those structures to the data of experience. Generally speaking, adaptation presupposes an interaction between subject and object, such that the first can incorporate the second into itself while also taking account of its particularities; and the more differentiated and the more complementary that assimilation and that accommodation are, the more thorough the adaptation.

The characteristic of childhood is precisely that it has to find this state of balance by means of a series of exercises or behavior patterns that are *sui generis,* by means of a continuous structuring activity beginning from a state of chaotic nondifferentiation between subject and object. This means, in effect, that at the very beginning of its mental development the child is pulled in opposite directions by two tendencies that have still not been brought into harmony with one another and are still relatively undifferentiated, insofar as they have not yet found their equilibrium with regard to one another. Firstly, it is perpetually obliged to accommodate its sensorimotor, or intellectual, organs to external reality, to the particularities of things, about which it has everything to learn. And this continuous process of accommodation—which is extended in the form of imitation when the subject's movements are sufficiently applicable to the characteristics of the object—constitutes one primary necessity of its action. Secondly, however—and this is something that has generally been less understood, except in fact by the practitioners and theorists of the new school—in order to accommodate its activity to the properties of things, the child needs to assimilate them and, in a very real sense, to incorporate them into itself. Things have no interest in the initial stage of mental life except insofar as they constitute fuel for activity proper, and this continuous assimilation of the external world into the self, although antithetic in direction to accommodation, is so intimately fused with it during the earliest stages that the child is at first unable to establish any clear-cut dividing line between its own activity and external reality, between subject and object.

However theoretical they may appear, these considerations are fundamental where schooling is concerned. For assimilation in its purest form—which is to say as long as it has not yet been brought into equilibrium with the process of accommodation to reality—is in effect nothing other than play; and play, which is one of the most characteristic infantile activities, has in fact found a use in the new techniques of education for young infants that remains inexplicable unless one clarifies the significance of this function in relation to the child's mental life as a whole and to its intellectual adaptation.

Play

Play is a typical case of the forms of behavior neglected by the traditional school because it appears to them to be devoid of functional significance. In current educational theory it is no more than a form of relaxation or a reaction brought on by an excess of energy. But this over-simple view explains neither the importance that young children attribute to their games nor, above all, the invariability of form that children's games assume—symbolism and fiction, for example.

After studying animals at play, Karl Groos arrived at a totally different conception of such behavior according to which play is a preparatory exercise, useful in the physical development of the organism. And just as the games of animals constitute a method of exercising particular instincts, such as fighting and hunting instincts, so the child when it plays is developing its perceptions, its intelligence, its impulses toward experiment, its social instincts, etc. This is why play is such a powerful lever in the learning process of very young children, to such an extent that whenever anyone can succeed in transforming their first steps in reading, or arithmetic, or spelling into a game, you will see children become passionately absorbed in those occupations, which are ordinarily presented as dreary chores.

Karl Groos' interpretation, however, which goes no further than a simple functional description, only acquires its full significance to the degree in which it is reinforced by the notion of assimilation. During the first year, for example, alongside the behavioral patterns of adaptation proper, during which the child attempts to grasp whatever it sees—to rock, shake, rub, etc.—it is easy enough to distinguish other forms of behavior that are simply a kind of exercise, characterized by the fact that their objects have no interest whatever in themselves but are assimilated into those forms of activity proper purely and simply as functional raw material. In such cases, which must be looked upon as the origin of play, the behavior patterns develop by functioning—in conformity with the general law of functional assimilation—and the objects on which they bear have no other significance for the infant than that of providing an opportunity for that exercise. In its sensorimotor origin play is nothing more than a pure assimilation of reality into the self, in the double sense of the term: in the biological sense of functional assimilation—which explains why these game-exercises really develop the organs and the behavior patterns—and in the psychological sense of incorporating objects into activity.

As for play at a higher level, that of imaginative and symbolic games, there is no doubt that Karl Groos failed to explain it adequately, since fiction in the child goes far beyond simple pre-exercise of particular instincts. Playing with dolls does not serve solely to develop the maternal instinct, but also provides a symbolic representation of all the realities the child has so far experienced but not yet assimilated in a form that it can relive and therefore vary according to its needs. So that in this respect symbolic play, like exercise play, is also to be explained as an assimilation of reality into the self: it is individual thought in its purest form; in its content, it is the unfolding and flowering of the self and a realization of desires, as opposed to rational socialized thought which adapts the self to reality and expresses shared truths; in its structure, the symbol in play is to the individual what the verbal sign is to society.

Play then, in its two essential forms of sensorimotor exercise and symbolism, is an assimilation of reality into activity proper, providing the latter with its necessary sustenance and transforming reality in accordance with the self's complex of needs. This is why the active methods of infant education all require that the children should be provided with suitable equipment, so that in playing they shall come to assimilate intellectual realities which would otherwise remain outside the infantile intelligence.

Although assimilation is necessary to adaptation, it nevertheless constitutes only one aspect of it. The complete adaptation that it is childhood's task to achieve consists in a progressive synthesis of assimilation with accommodation. This is why, in the course of its own internal development, the play of small children is gradually transformed into adapted constructions requiring an ever increasing amount of what is in effect work, to such an extent that in the infant classes of an active school every kind of spontaneous transition may be observed between play and work. But above all, from the very earliest months of life, the synthesis of assimilation and accommodation takes place through the agency of the intelligence itself, whose unifying labor increases with age and whose real activity it is now time to emphasize to the full, since it is upon this notion that the new education is ultimately based.

Intelligence

For classical psychology, intelligence was to be conceived of as either as a faculty given once and for all, and susceptible of knowing reality, or as a system of associations mechanically acquired under the pressure exerted by things. Hence, we have seen the importance attributed by older educational theories to receptivity and the furnishing of the memory. Today, on the other hand, the most advanced experimental psychology recognizes the existence of an intelligence going beyond the mechanisms of association and habit and attributes to that intelligence an authentic activity, not merely the faculty of knowing.

For some, this activity consists of trials and errors, at first practical and external, then becoming interiorized in the form of a mental construction of hypotheses and a process of research controlled by the representations themselves (Claparède). For others, it implies a continuous reorganization of the field of perception and a creative structuration (Kohler, etc.). But all these psychologists agree in accepting that intelligence begins by being practical, or sensorimotor, in nature before gradually interiorizing itself to become thought in the strict sense, and in recognizing that its activity is a continuous process of construction.

Study of the birth of intelligence during the first year of life seems to indicate that intellectual functioning takes the form of neither tentative groping nor of purely endogenous structuration but of a structuring activity that implies both forms elaborated by the subject and a perpetual adjustment of those forms to the data of experience. In other words, intelligence is adaptation in its highest form, the balance between a continuous assimilation of things to activity proper and the accommodation of those assimilative schemata to things themselves.

The result of this is that the child does not comprehend phenomena (for example spatial relations, causal relations, etc.) on the level of practical intelligence except by assimilating them to its motor activity, but having done so, in the reverse direction it accommodates those schemata of assimilation to the details of external facts. Similarly, the early stages of the child's thought display a constant assimilation of things to the action of the subject combined with a no less systematic accommodation of those schemata to its experience. Then, as assimilation becomes more and more closely combined with accommodation, the first of these is reduced to deductive activity itself, the second to experimentation, and the union of these two becomes that indissociable relation between deduction and experience that is the the characteristic of reason.

Conceived of in this way, infantile intelligence cannot be treated, any more than adult intelligence, by purely receptive educational methods. All intelligence is an adaptive process; all adaptation entails an assimilation of things into the mind, just as does the complementary process of accommodation. Thus all work on the part of the intelligence rests on an interest.

Interest is nothing other, in effect, than the dynamic aspect of assimilation. As Dewey demonstrated with such profundity, true interest appears when the self identifies itself with ideas or objects, when it finds in them a means of expression and they become a necessary form of fuel for its activity. When the active school requires that the student's effort should come from the student himself instead of being imposed, and that his intelligence should undertake authentic work instead of accepting pre-digested knowledge from outside, it is therefore simply asking that the laws of all intelligence should be respected. Even in the adult the intellect cannot function effectively, cannot provide an opportunity for an effort on the part of the entire personality, unless its object is assimilated by that personality instead of remaining exterior to it. And this is even truer in the case of the child, since in the child the assimilation into the self is not from the outset in equilibrium with the process of accommodation to things and hence necessitates a continuous play-exercise process alongside the adaptation proper.

The law of interest, which still controls the intellectual functioning of the adult, is therefore valid *a fortiori* for the child, whose interests are not coordinated and unified in the same way, thus excluding to an even greater extent than in us the possibility of heteronomous work on the part of the mind. Hence what Claparède calls the law of functional autonomy: "At each moment of its development, an animal being constitutes a functional unity, which is another way of saying that its capacities for reaction are adjusted to its needs" (*L'éducation fonctionnelle*).

As we have already noted, though the functioning of the mind is the same at all age levels, the particular mental structures are susceptible to variation with growth. The same is true of psychic realities as of organisms: the basic functions are constant, but they may be performed by different organs. And though the new education would have us treat the child as an autonomous being from the point of view of the functional conditions of its work, it also requires, on the other hand, that we should take account of its mentality from the structural point of view. That is its second notable originality.

For traditional education theory has always treated the child, in effect, as a small adult, as a being who reasons and feels just as we do while merely lacking our knowledge and experience. So that, since the child viewed in this way was no more than an ignorant adult, the educator's task was not so much to form its mind as simply to furnish it; the subject matter provided from outside was thought to be exercise enough in itself. But the problem becomes quite different as soon as one begins with the hypothesis of structural variations. If the child's thought is qualitatively different from our own, then the principal aim of education is to form its intellectual and moral reasoning power. And since that power cannot be formed from outside, the question is to find the most suitable methods and environment to help the child constitute it itself, in other words, to achieve coherence and objectivity on the intellectual plane and reciprocity on the moral plane.

It is therefore of fundamental importance for the new school to know what the structure of the child's thought is, and what the relations are between infantile and adult mentality. All the creators of the active school have had either a general intuition or precise information—relating to some particular point in child psychology—about the structural differences between childhood and the adult state. Rousseau was already affirming in his day that each age has its own ways of thinking; but this notion did not become a positive one until it was made so by twentieth-century psychology, thanks to its research into the child itself and also, in part, to the ideas of comparative psychology and sociology. Thus, in the United States, as a consequence of the researches of Stanley Hall and his school on the one hand, and of Dewey and his collaborators (I. King among others) on the other, a profound theoretician, J. M. Baldwin, was able to establish (though in an insufficiently experimental way, alas) the outline of a "genetic logic." Now the idea alone of such a discipline is full of significance: it shows how much we have become accustomed to thinking, in contrast to the beliefs of the nineteenth-century positivists and rationalists, that reason actually undergoes a structural development, and that the process it goes through during childhood is one of genuine construction. In Europe, the work of Decroly and Claparède on children's perceptions, of Stern on infantile language, and of K. Groos on play, not to mention the theories derived from certain famous studies of the primitive mentality or the Freudian analyses of symbolic thought, have all led to analogous ideas. And it seems to me necessary to deal with this problem here, albeit briefly, since it has considerable bearing on the evaluation to be made of the new methods of education.

Adult Logic, Child Logic

Where intellectual education is concerned, the crucial question is that of the child's logic.

If the child reasons in the same way as we do, then the traditional school is justified in presenting the subject matter to be taught in the same way as though it were simply a matter of giving lectures to adults. But we need do no more than analyze the results of arithmetic or geometry lessons in primary schools according to age groups in order to become aware, from the very start, of the enormous hiatus that exists between an adult theory, even an elementary one, and its comprehension by children below the age of eleven to twelve.

A first difference that should be emphasized, one that would suffice in itself to justify the efforts of the active school, is that concerning the relationship between gnostic, or reflexive, intelligence and practical, or sensorimotor, intelligence. When a sufficiently high level of mental development is reached, practice is seen as an application of theory. Thus our industries, for example, have long since passed the empirical stage and now benefit daily from the applications of science. Similarly, in the normal individual, the solution of a problem of practical intelligence results either from lucid theoretical representations or from a process of empirical groping, in which it is not difficult to discern the constant influence of previous theoretically established knowledge. This is why the traditional school of education is prejudiced in favor of theoretical principles: children are taught grammar, for example, before they have had practice in speaking, and the rules of arithmetic before they have had any problems to solve, etc.

The fact is, however, that before any kind of language, and consequently before any conceptual or reflexive thought, there develops in the baby a sensorimotor, or practical, intelligence that is able, unaided, to advance far enough in the conquest of reality to construct the essentials of space and object, causality and time—in short, succeeds even at that early age in organizing a whole solid and coherent universe on the level of action (J. Piaget, *La naissance de l'intelligence chez l'enfant* and *La construction du réel chez l'enfant*). And even when it has reached school age, the child still provides evidence of a practical intelligence serving as a substructure for its conceptual intelligence, and the mechanisms of the former appear to be independent of the latter and entirely original (André Rey, *L'intelligence pratique chez l'enfant*).

Moreover, though the relationship between these two types of intelligence has still not been clearly established in its details, we can nevertheless say with certainty that, in infants, practical intelligence precedes reflexive intelligence, and that the latter consists, to a large extent, in achieving a conscious grasp of the results of the former. At the very least, we can affirm that the reflexive intelligence cannot succeed in creating anything new, in its own sphere of signs and concepts, except on condition that its constructions are solidly based on foundations laid down by the practical intelligence.

For example, a child's spontaneous grasp of the physical world will enable it to succeed in predicting phenomena long before it can explain them (the perception of laws by the practical intelligence preceding a grasp of causality, which necessitates reflexive deduction), but the correct explanation consists in achieving a progressive conscious awareness of the motives that guided the prediction (J. Piaget, *La causalité physique chez l'enfant*).

To resume, then, we find that practical adaptation in infants, far from being an application of conceptual knowledge, constitutes, on the contrary, the first stage of knowledge itself and the necessary condition of all subsequent reflexive knowledge.

This is why the active methods of educating infants succeed so much better than other methods in the teaching of abstract subjects such as arithmetic and geometry. When the child has already manipulated numbers or surfaces, as it were, before knowing them through the agency of thought, the notion that it acquires of them subsequently consists of a genuine bringing into consciousness of already familiar schemata of action, and not, as in the ordinary methods, of a verbal concept accompanied by formal exercises devoid of interest and lacking any previous experimental substructure. Practical intelligence is therefore one of the essential psychological data upon which active education rests. But in order to prevent any misunderstanding, it should be noted in passing that the term "active" is used here in a particular sense. As Claparède has said (*L'éducation fonctionnelle,* p. 205), the term activity is ambiguous and can be taken either in the sense of functional behavior based on interest or in the sense of "performance" referring to some external operation of a motor nature. In fact, only the first of these two kinds of activity characterizes the active school at every level (for one can be active in the first sense even in pure thought), whereas the second kind of activity is indispensable in the highest degree solely in infants and diminishes in importance with age.

This reversal of the relationship between practical, or sensorimotor, intelligence and reflexive intelligence, however, is far from being the only structural difference distinguishing the child's thought from our own. In the conceptual sphere proper there are several remarkable particularities to be noted that are equally as important from the point of view of educational practice. These involve at least three essential domains in the logical structure of thought: formal principles, the structure of classes or concepts, and the structure of relations.

And where these three things are concerned there seems to be one observed fact from which it would be as well to start: before the age of ten or eleven the child is hardly capable of any kind of formal reasoning; which is to say, of deductions based upon merely assumed data and not on observed facts (J. Piaget, *Le jugement et le raisonnement chez l'enfant*).

For instance, confronted with the usual mathematical problems, one of the difficulties young children experience is that of limiting themselves to the terms of those problems instead of resorting to concrete memories drawn from their personal experience. Generally speaking, it is impossible for a child before the age of about ten to understand the hypothetico-deductive as opposed to the empirical truth of mathematics; and, moreover, there does seem to be room for astonishment that classical pedagogy should in this field impose on schoolboys a way of reasoning that the Greeks achieved by dint of great struggle only after centuries of empirical arithmetic and geometry. Moreover, the analyses we have succeeded in making of certain purely verbal reasoning processes also demonstrate this same difficulty in coping with formal reasoning before the age of ten or eleven. And this being so, there seems good reason to ask oneself whether perhaps the child simply does not possess as we do the principles of identity, of noncontradiction, of deduction, etc., and to pose the same problems with regard to its mentality as Lévy-Bruhl did when studying noncivilized tribes.

It seems clear, moreover, that our answer should take into account the distinction already observed between functions and structures. It is undeniable, from the functional point of view, that the child is already striving toward coherence: that is in the nature of all thought, and the child's obeys the same functional laws as ours. But the forms of coherence that satisfy the child are not the same as those we require, and it may be said—if it is a question of the clearly defined concepts necessary for that specialized structure, formal coherence of thought—that it does not achieve them right away. It frequently reasons in a way that is, to us, contradictory.

This brings us to the infantile method of establishing classes or concepts. The almost exclusive use that traditional education makes of language in order to act upon the pupil implies that the child elaborates its concepts in the same way as we do, and that a term-for-term correspondence is thus established between the ideas of the teacher and those of the pupil. In fact, however, the existence of verbalism, that dismal scholastic fact—a proliferation of pseudo-ideas loosely hooked onto a string of words lacking all real meaning—is fairly conclusive proof that the workings of this mechanism are not without their snags, and explains one of the fundamental reasons for the active school's reaction against the receptive school.

The matter is not a hard one to understand. Adult concepts, codified in intellectual language and handled by professionals in the field of oral exposition and debate, constitute mental instruments whose essential uses are, on the one hand to put knowledge already acquired into systematic form, and on the other to facilitate communication and mental exchanges between individuals. In the child, however, practical intelligence still largely predominates over gnostic intelligence; research precedes collated knowledge; and above all, the effort of thought remains for a long while incommunicable, and therefore less socialized, than with us. With the child, a concept therefore depends on the sensorimotor schemata for its origin, and continues for many years to be controlled by the process of assimilating reality into the self rather than by the discursive rules of socialized thought. This being so, it proceeds rather by means of syncretic assimilation than by logical generalization. If we try to subject children younger than ten or eleven to experiments involving the concept-constituting operations that logicians have termed logical addition and multiplication, then we shall find that the subjects experience an invariable difficulty in applying them. Analysis of the child's verbal comprehension, moreover, shows the same processes of all-embracing and syncretic fusion that Decroly and Claparède observed in the sphere of perception. In short, the child continues for a long while to have no grasp of the hierarchical systems of clearly delimited concepts, of clear-cut inclusions and disjunctions; it therefore cannot immediately attain to formal coherence, and reasons by means of that sort of ill-regulated deduction that lacks either true generality or true necessity, which W. Stern has called transduction.

As for what the logicians have termed relational logic, the difference in that field between the child's thought and formal reasoning is even more glaring. Alongside predicative propositions there exist, as we know, propositions comprising between them terms that are not mutually inclusive; this system of relations is more fundamental than that of concepts, since the former serves in the constitution of the latter.

In the child, however, relations certainly appear to be of a primitive kind in the genetic order; they are at work as early as the sensorimotor phase; but their manipulation on the level of reflexive intelligence remains difficult for a long time: individual thought begins, in effect, by judging everything from its own point of view—and by regarding as absolute characteristics that it will later come to recognize as being relative. Give some young children three visually identical boxes of which the first is lighter than the second and heavier than the third, then ask them which is the heaviest; they will often reason like this: the two first are light, the first and the third are heavy, therefore the third is the heaviest and the second the lightest.

The child's thought functions like our own and presents the same special functions of coherence, classification, explanation, relational arrangement, etc. But the particular logical structures that fulfill these functions are susceptible of development and variation. In consequence, the practitioners and theorists of the new school have come to regard it as necessary to present the subject matter of education to the child in accordance with rules quite different from those to which our discursive and analytic minds attribute the monopoly of lucidity and simplicity. There are many examples that could be given of this, particularly in Decroly's method, which is based on the ideas of "aggregation," or syncretism.

The Stages of Intellectual Development

Here we encounter a fundamental problem: that of the mechanisms themselves by which the mind achieves its development. Let us suppose that the structural variations of the child's thought are determined from within, bound by an immutable order of succession and an unvarying chronology, each stage beginning at its appointed moment and occupying a precisely ordained period of the child's life; suppose, in a word, that the development of individual thought is comparable to an embryology obeying strict hereditary rules, then the consequences would be incalculable for education: the teacher would be wasting his time and his effort attempting to speed up the development of his students, and the problem would simply be that of finding out what knowledge corresponded to each stage and then to present it in a manner assimilable by the mental structure of the age level in question.

Inversely, if the development of reason depended uniquely on individual experience and on the influences wielded by the physical and social environment, then the school, while still taking the structure of primitive consciousness into account, could very well accelerate that development to the extent of telescoping the stages and identifying the child with the adult in the shortest possible time.

Every variety of opinion has been held as far as the mechanism of mental development is concerned though all of them have not given rise to durable educational applications. This is precisely because scholastic life is a systematic experiment that makes it possible to study the influence of environment on mental growth and, in consequence, to discard excessively rash interpretations.

For example, the psychic life of the child has been conceived of as a continuous series of succcessive periods determined by heredity and corresponding to the periods of human history. It was in this way that Stanley Hall, influenced by certain biological notions current in the late nineteenth century—supposed onto-phylogenetic parallelism, or the theory of hereditarily acquired characteristics— interpreted the evolution of children's games as a systematic recapitulation of ancestral activities. This theory had its influence on several educational theorists, though without producing any noteworthy applications; nor has it left any vestiges from the psychological point of view, and recent research carried out in the United States, relating the sequence of games to age groups, has shown that little Americans are becoming less and less concerned with ancestral activities and are increasingly deriving inspiration for their play from the spectacles offered by the contemporary social environment (Mrs. Curti, *Child Psychology*).

Meanwhile the opposite idea, that intellectual development owes a considerable amount to an internal maturation independent of the external environment, has been gaining ground. Long periods of practice are necessary in order to learn to walk before the maturation of the nerve centers involved; but prevent the baby from making any attempt to walk before the optimum moment arrives, and at its first attempt the ability to walk will be acquired almost instantaneously. Similarly, the research done by Gesell on identical twins, and the work of Buhler with Albanian infants—who are kept in swaddling clothes until very late and then develop like forest fires the moment they are unwrapped—show that even in those mental acquisitions most apparently influenced by individual experience and external environment the maturation of the nervous system still plays a fundamental role. Indeed, Buhler even goes so far as to accept that the stages of mental development she has established constitute necessary phases and correspond to invariable chronological ages. This is not the moment, however, to argue the exaggeration of such a conception, especially since it has not, to my knowledge, given rise to any systematic educational applications.

Others, on the contrary, have conceived the intellectual development of the child as being due to experience alone. According to Mrs. Isaacs (*The Intellectual Growth of Young Children*), a worthy inheritor in this respect of English empiricism, the hereditary mental structure of the child does no more than lead it to record the lessons of reality; or rather—since even empiricism believes today in an activity of the mind—the child is impelled by its own inner tendencies to undertake a continual organizing process of its experiences and to retain the results for use in subsequent attempts.

This is not the place for a demonstration of how far, from the psychological point of view, such an empiricism still implies, despite everything, the notion of an assimilative structure developing with age. I shall limit myself to observing that this doctrine, in its educational applications, results in an optimism no less in degree than if the development were wholly determined by factors of internal maturation. And indeed, in the little Malting House school in Cambridge, Mrs. Isaacs and her collaborators did in fact abstain rigorously from all adult intervention, on the theory that it is precisely adult instruction and its clumsy mistakes that prevent children from working. What they did do was to present their pupils with what amounted to a genuine, fully-equipped laboratory so that they could then be left to organize their experiments themselves. The children, ranging from three to eight years in age, had the greatest possible number of raw materials and instruments at their disposal: test tubes, boiling tubes, Bunsen burners, etc., not to mention all the apparatus for natural history study. The results were by no means without interest: the children, even at that early age, did not remain inactive in this environment so well equipped for research, but undertook all sorts of manipulations that were evidently of passionate interest to them; they were really learning to observe and to reason as they observed, both individually and in common. But the impression that my visit to this astonishing experimental school made upon me was twofold. On the one hand, even these exceptionally favorable circumstances were insufficient to erase the various features of the child's mental structure and did no more than accelerate their development. On the other hand, some form of systematization applied by the adult would perhaps not have been wholly harmful to the pupils. Needless to say, in order to draw any conclusion it would have been necessary to pursue the experiment up to the end of the subjects' secondary studies; but it is highly possible that the result would have demonstrated, to a greater degree than these particular educationalists would wish, the necessity for a rational, deductive activity to give a meaning to scientific experiment, and the necessity also, in order to establish such a reasoning activity in the child, for a surrounding social structure entailing not merely cooperation among the children but also cooperation with adults.

As for those new methods of education that have had the most durable success, and which without doubt constitute the foundation of tomorrow's active school, they all more or less draw their inspiration from a doctrine of the golden mean, allowing room both for internal structural maturation and also for the influences of experience and of the social and physical environment. As opposed to the traditional school, which denies the existence of the first of these factors by identifying the child with the adult from the outset, these methods take the stages of mental development into account; but, as opposed to those theories based on the idea of purely hereditary maturation, they also believe in the possibility of influencing that development.

The Value of the Developmental Stages in Educational Science

How then are we to interpret these laws and these stages of intellectual development from the point of view of the school? As an example, let us take the development of causality in the child (Piaget, *La représentation du monde chez l'enfant* and *La causalité physique chez l'enfant*).

When we question children of different ages about the principal natural phenomena in which they feel a spontaneous interest, we receive replies that differ very widely according to the age groups of the subjects questioned. In very young children one finds all sorts of conceptions whose importance diminishes noticeably with age: things are endowed with life and intentionality, they are capable of movement of their own accord, and the purpose of those movements is both to ensure the harmony of the world and to serve mankind. In the oldest children we no longer find anything that differs very much from adult representations of order and causality, with the exception of one or two vestiges of previous stages. Between these extremes on the other hand, in children of from about eight to eleven, we find a great many forms of explanations intermediate between the artificialist animism of the very young and the mechanism of the older subjects. As a particular example of this there is, for instance, a fairly systematic form of dynamism of which several manifestations are reminiscent of the physics of Aristotle, and which is an extension of the primitive physics of the young child while at the same time providing a foundation for more rational connections.

Such a development of response would seem to bear witness to a structural transformation of thought with age. It is true, of course, that the same results have not been observed everywhere, and this inconsistency of reactions must itself be carefully recorded for use in the final interpretation of the procedure. Nevertheless, if one compares the reactions of small children in general to those of older children it is impossible not to accept the existence of a maturing process; scientific causality is not innate, but constructed little by little, and this process of construction presupposes not only an adaptation of the mind to reality but also a correction of the initial egocentrism of thought (of the assimilation into the self discussed earlier).

From this general observation, however, to an acceptance of inflexible stages characterized by invariable chronological age limits and by a permanent thought content is a long way indeed. To begin with, the characteristic ages one can achieve, even when the procedure includes a large number of children, are never more than averages; so that their succession, although real in an overall sense, does not exclude either telescoping or even momentary individual regressions. Secondly, there are all sorts of overlaps when one passes from one particular test to another: a child that belongs in one particular stage as far as one particular question of causality is concerned may very well have moved on to the next stage with regard to some neighboring causal question. Just as in science a new conception may appear in one sphere without penetrating for some years into the other disciplines, so a particular form of behavior or a recently acquired notion does not become general right away, and each problem entails its own particular difficulties. These overlaps in extension, if such a phrase may be employed, probably exclude the possibility of establishing generally applicable stage limits, except during the first two or three years of existence.

In the third place, there are also, as it were, overlaps in comprehension: the same notion may appear on the sensorimotor, or practical, level long before becoming the object of a conscious elucidation or of reflection (as we saw earlier with relational logic). This lack of synchronism between the different levels of action and thought complicates our picture of the developmental stages even further. Finally, and above all (for it would be impossible to emphasize this point too strongly), each stage of development is characterized much less by a fixed thought content than by a certain power, a certain potential activity, capable of achieving such and such a result according to the environment in which the child lives.

Here we are touching upon a question that is all-important, not only for the new education and psychopedagogy but also for child psychology in general; it is one that raises difficulties analogous to those of genetic biology.

It is well-known that many problems concerning heredity remained confused until distinction was made—among animal and vegetable variations—between the genotypes or endogenous hereditary variations and the phenotypes or nonhereditary variations related to the environment. Now any direct measurement we make is always of the phenotypes, since an organism always lives in a certain environment, while the genotype is simply the invariable factor common to all the phenotypes of the same pure strain. But this invariable, although it entails abstraction on the part of the intelligence, is what in fact enables us to understand the mechanism of variation. Similarly in psychology: the child's thought (though no more so than that of the adult) cannot ever be captured in itself and independently of the environment.

The child at a given stage will produce different work and give variable replies to analogous questions according to his family or school environment, according to who is questioning him, etc. Thus we can never obtain any thing more from experiments than sorts of mental phenotypes, and it will always remain bad practice to look upon such or such a reaction as an absolute characteristic, such as the permanent content of a given stage. However, by comparing the replies given by children of the same age group in a variety of environments with the replies provided by subjects in other age groups in the same environments it does become apparent, nevertheless, that common features can be determined and that these general characteristics are in fact an index of the potential activity differentiating each stage from the others.

Although we cannot at present fix with any certainty the boundary between the contribution of the mind's structural maturation and that of the child's individual experience or the influences exerted by his physical and social environment, it does nevertheless seem that we should accept both that these two factors are constantly at work and that development is a product of their continuous interaction. From the point of view of schooling, this means, in the first place, that we must recognize the existence of a process of mental development; that all intellectual raw material is not invariably assimilable at all ages; that we should take into account the particular interests and needs of each stage. It also means, in the second place, that environment can play a decisive role in the development of the mind; that the thought contents of the stages and the ages at which they occur are not immutably fixed; that sound methods can therefore increase the students' efficiency and even accelerate their spiritual growth without making it any the less sound.

The Child's Social Life

The question of environmental influence on development, and the fact that the reactions characterizing the various stages of it are always related as much to the particular surroundings and atmosphere as to the organic maturation of the mind, now bring us, at the end of this brief exposition, to an examination of the psychopedagogic problem of the social relationships characteristic of childhood. And this is one of the points upon which the new school and the traditional school are divided in the most significant manner.

The traditional school hardly offers scope for more than one type of social relationship: the action of the teacher upon the pupil. It is without doubt true, of course, that a school class constitutes a true group, whatever the methods applied in its work, and schools have always approved of the comradeship and the rules of mutual aid and justice that are established within such a society. But it is also true, if we except play and games periods, that this social life developed among the children themselves is never employed in the classroom itself; the erroneously named collective exercises are in reality no more than a mere juxtaposition of individual work carried out in the same place. The teacher's action on the pupil is therefore everything. Moreover, since the teacher is endowed with both intellectual and moral authority, and since the pupil owes him or her obedience, this social relationship constitutes an absolutely

typical case of what sociologists term constraint, it being understood that the coercive character of such constraint becomes apparent solely in cases of nonsubmission and that, in its normal
functioning, it may be gentle and easily accepted by the pupil.

The new methods of education, on the other hand, have from the
outset allotted an essential place to the social life that develops
among the children themselves. As early as the first experiments
made by Dewey and Decroly, the children were free to work with
one another, to collaborate in intellectual research as much as in
the establishing of a moral discipline; this team work and this self
government have become essential ingredients of active school
practice. And it will be of value to go into the problems raised by
this infantile social life.

From the point of view of inherited behavior—which is to say of
the social instincts, or of that society which Durkheim referred to
as being internal to the individual, because it is bound up with the
organism's psychobiological constitution—the child is social almost from the day of its birth. It smiles at people in its second
month and seeks to make contact with others (and indeed we all
know how demanding babies are already on this point, and how
much they need company if not accustomed to regular periods of
solitary activity). But alongside these internal social tendencies
there is also the society that is external to individuals, which is to
say the totality of those relationships being established between
them from the outside: language, intellectual exchanges, moral or
legal action—in short, everything that is handed on from generation to generation and that constitutes the essential foundation
of human society, as opposed to animal societies based upon instinct.

From this point of view, and despite the fact that it possesses
urges toward sympathy and imitation from the very first, the child
has everything to learn. It starts, in effect, from a purely individual
state—that of the first months of existence during which no exchange with others is possible—and ends by undergoing a progressive socialization that in fact never ends. At the start, it knows
nothing of either rules or signs and must therefore go through a

process of gradual adaptation—composed both of assimilation of others to itself and of accommodation of itself to others—that will enable it to master two essential properties of external society: mutual comprehension based on speech, and a communal discipline based on standards of reciprocity.

So that from this point of view (though solely from this point of view, that is, of external society), we may say that the child proceeds from an initial state of unconscious egocentrism that is correlative to its nondifferentiation from the group. On the one hand, small children (and this is true from the second half of the first year onward) not only seek to make contact with others but also constantly imitate them, thus giving evidence in this respect of a very high degree of suggestibility; and this is the form taken on the social level by that aspect of adaptation that we designated earlier by the term "accommodation," and of which the equivalent in the physical world is the phenomenist acceptance of the outward aspects of experience. But on the other hand, and by the same token, the child is also constantly assimilating others to itself, which is to say that being unable to penetrate below the surface of their behavior and their motives it cannot understand them except by reducing everything to its own point of view, and by projecting its own thoughts and desires into them. As long as it has not mastered both the social instruments of exchange or mutual comprehension and the discipline that subjects the self to the rules of reciprocity, it is quite evident that the child has no choice but to believe itself the center of both the social and the physical worlds, and to judge everything by means of egocentric assimilation to itself. But then, as it gradually comes to understand others in the same way as itself, and to subject its will and its thought to rules whose coherence is sufficient to make such an arduous objectivity possible, it succeeds simultaneously both in emerging from itself and in becoming aware of its self, in other words, in situating itself from the outside among others while at the same time discovering both its own personality and that of everyone else.

In short, the social development of the child proceeds from egocentrism toward reciprocity, from assimilation into a self still not conscious of itself to mutual comprehension leading to the constitution of personality, from chaotic nondifferentiation within the group to a differentiation based upon disciplined organization.

The Effects of the Initial Egocentrism

Let us begin by examining the effects of this initial egocentrism, which may be observed, first of all, in young children's behavior.

At play, and in schools where the children are left free to work either individually or together, small children display a very characteristic mode of behavior. They like being together, and often deliberately split up into groups of two or three, but even so they do not generally attempt to coordinate their efforts: each acts for itself alone, with or without mutual assimilation. For example, in a collective game such as marbles, even as late as five or six years old, each child applies the rules in its own way and everyone wins at the same time. In symbolic or construction games we find exactly the same mixture of contact, blatant imitation and unconscious isolation. This is why team work methods always fail with very young children.

The child's language in such situations is also often significant. At the Maison des Petits in Geneva we have observed a very high proportion of collective monologues in children from three to six years of age during which each child talks for its own benefit without really listening to the others (Piaget, *Le langage et la pensée chez l'enfant*). In other environments observation has yielded a lesser incidence of such egocentric language, or even a relative absence of these manifestations (Delacroix, *Le langage de l'enfant*). It is nevertheless evident, I believe, that the infant soliloquy or collective monologue constitutes the type or norm of these phenotypical characteristics of one stage, which is to say that they relate not only to the child but also to the environment in which it is active. And it is in fact true, firstly, that these phenomena are observed only in children below the age of seven to eight and not in older children, which is fairly sufficient evidence that we are dealing with a characteristic exclusive to the earlier stages. And secondly, this characteristic manifests itself only in certain environments; it can be reduced or developed according to the scholastic or family atmosphere, which is to say according to the action exercised by adults.

It is above all from the intellectual point of view, however, that egocentrism is worthy of attention and constitutes a phenomenon of general importance. We have already seen that it is the continuous assimilation of the world to the child's individual activity that explains play.

Symbolic play in particular would be incomprehensible without this assimilation of reality to thought, since it explains both the satisfaction of those desires characteristic of the imagination at play and also the symbolic structure of play as opposed to the conceptual and verbal structure of socialized thought. Play is thus the most characteristic type of egocentric thought, which is thought for which the external universe ceases to have any objective importance, thus becoming wholly malleable to the interests of the self and merely serving as an instrument for its development. Now, if symbolic play is nothing other than individual thought pursuing its own unfettered satisfaction by assimilating things to its own activity, then the child's egocentrism is revealed in the process of adaptation itself. Which is, after all, natural enough, since adaptation is an equilibrium between assimilation and accommodation, and since that equilibrium implies a long period of structuration before its two processes can become complementary.

Thus, the two aspects of the child's logic, which we described earlier as being characteristic of its mental structure during the first stages of development, exist in a state of close interdependence with egocentrism. If the child experiences such difficulty in handling relations on the level of thought, whereas its sensorimotor activity is already adapted to deal with the relations between things, this is because relativity implies reciprocity of viewpoints and because, before it has accustomed its mind to such reciprocity by means of inter-individual exchanges and coöperation, the individual must remain the prisoner of his own point of view, which he naturally looks upon as absolute. Furthermore, if the child has so much difficulty in constituting genuine concepts and handling the operations of the logic of classes, that is because discussion and the discursive necessities of intellectual exchange are indispensable for the education of the analytic mind and in order to bring the mind to recognize the value of fixed definitions and clear concepts. Generally speaking, the formal rules of logic constitute a moral of thought that cooperation and the respect for truth cooperation implies are alone capable of establishing.

The Processes of Socialization

Thus, in every sphere—and this is something even easier to establish from a moral than from an intellectual point of view—the child remains egocentric to the degree in which it has still not adapted to external social realities. This egocentrism constitutes one of the aspects of each of its mental structures. How then does the child succeed in adapting itself to social life, or, to put it another way, what are the processes of socialization?

Here the originality of the new methods of education becomes very apparent. The traditional school reduced all socialization, whether intellectual or moral, to a mechanism of constraint. The active school, on the contrary, makes a careful distinction in almost all its achievements between two processes that have very different results and become complementary only with much care and tact: the constraint exercised by the adult and the cooperation of the children with each other. The constraint exercised by the adult achieves results that are all the more considerable in that they answer to very profound tendencies in the child's mentality.

In effect, the child experiences for the adult in general, though particularly for its parents, that essential emotion, composed of mingled fear and affection, called respect; and as P. Bovet has shown (Les conditions de l'obligation de conscience, Année psychologique, 1912), respect derives neither from the law as such, as Kant thought, nor, as Durkheim would have it, from the social group embodied in individuals; it constitutes a primary fact in the affective relations between the infant and the adults surrounding it, and explains at one and the same time both the child's obedience and the constitution of imperative rules. And indeed, to the degree in which a person is respected by the child, so the orders and instructions that person gives are experienced as compulsory. The genesis of the sense of duty is thus to be explained by respect, and not vice versa, which is a fair indication of the essential significance of the adult's action on the child.

Given that in the earliest stage of development the adult is thus the source of all morality and all truth, this situation, however, is not without its concomitant dangers. From the intellectual point of view, for example, the prestige the adult possesses in the child's eyes means that the latter accepts all affirmations issuing from the teacher as unquestionable, that authority, in other words, dispenses with the need for reflection. And since its egocentric attitude is already impelling the child's mind toward precisely such uncontrolled affirmation, respect for the adult often succeeds in consolidating the child's egocentrism instead of correcting it, by simply replacing a belief in self with a belief based on authority, instead of leading the way toward the reflection and the critical discussion that help to constitute reason and that can only be developed by cooperation and genuine intellectual exchange. From the moral point of view the danger is the same. Corresponding to the verbalism of intellectual submission there is a sort of moral realism: good and bad are simply conceived of as being that which is or is not in conformity with adult rules. This essentially heteronomous morality of obedience leads to all sorts of distortions. Since it is incapable of leading the child toward that autonomy of the personal conscience that constitutes the morality of the good as opposed to that of pure duty, it thus fails to prepare the child for an acceptance of the essential values of contemporary society. This explains the efforts of the new educational theory to supplement the deficiencies of externally imposed discipline with an internal discipline based upon the social life of the children themselves.

For not only are the children capable, within their own societies and particularly in their collective games, of imposing rules upon themselves that they often respect with more conviction and conscientiousness than some orders issued by adults, but also they are all individually aware that parallel to their classroom discipline, and more or less clandestine in nature, there exists a whole system of mutual aid based upon a "special understanding," as well as a sense *sui generis* of justice. The new methods all tend to employ these collective energies rather than ignore them or allow them to become transformed into hostile forces.

In this repect the cooperation among the children themselves has an importance as great as that of adult action. From the intellectual point of view, it is such cooperation that is most apt to encourage real exchange of thought and discussion, which is to say, all the forms of behavior capable of developing the critical attitude of mind, objectivity, and discursive reflection. From the moral point of view it results in a real exercise of the principles of behavior, and not solely in a submission to external constraint. In other words, social life, introduced into the classroom through the agency of effective collaboration among the students and the autonomous discipline of the group, implies the very ideal of the activity we have already described as being characteristic of the new school: it is morality in action, just as "active" work is intelligence as act. And even more than this, cooperation leads to the formation of a number of particular and interrelated values such as those of justice based on equality and those of "organic" interdependence.

Needless to say, except in certain extreme cases, the tendency of the new methods of education is not to eliminate the social action of the teacher, but rather to achieve a reconciliation between respect for the adult and cooperation among the children, and, as far as possible, to reduce the constraint exercised by the former in order to transform it into a higher form of cooperation.

Index

philosophy: and knowledge, 55–57; teaching of, 55, 57–60; relation of, to psychology, sociology, scientific spirit, and Marxism, 57–58

physical experience, and experiment, 37–39

Piaget, Jean, 25, 52, 56, 162, 163, 170, 176

Piaget Rediscovered, 54

Piéron, H., 104, 108

Pioneer centers in the U.S.S.R., 68

planning, educational, 19–20, 85–90

Planning in Education, 90

Plato, 56

play, functional significance of, 155–157

Poland, 61, 85, 89, 92–93, 115

praxis, 67

pre-school education, 96–99

primary education, primary schools, 11, 32, 54, 83, 101, 110, 111; *see also* elementary, programs, training of teachers, *and* vocational

problems of teaching, central, 12–14

Process of Education, The, 53

programmed teaching, 77–80

programs of primary and secondary education, 109–112

"proportional" operations, 33

psychic activity, 145

psychological examination, 109

psychological training, 129–130

Psychologie de l'enfant et pédagogie expérimentale, 54

psychologists, school, 103–106

psychology, 24, 39, 158; teaching of, 57; scholastic, 109; development of modern, 145–147; and new methods of education, 148–150; *see also* child psychology, psychological, *and* psychologists

psychosociology, 143

Pythagoras, 56, 73

qualificative psychological examination, *see* psychological examination

Quebec, Province of, 97; *see also* Parent Commission *and* Parent Report

Rabelais, François, 139

reading, experimental methods of teaching, 21–24

receptive methods, 66

reconstruction of actions, 31–32

recruiting teachers, difficulty of, 11

"reinforcements," external, 75

relational logic, 165

research institutes and academies, 14–17

respect by children, nature of, 178–180

responses or reactions, nature of, 170–171

restructuration in language, 40

results of educational techniques, ignorance of, 5–6

Reuchlin,104; and psychological tests, 109

Revue de métaphysique et de morale, 139

Rey, André, 162

Ripple, R. E., 54

Rockastle, V. N., 54

Rossello, P., 20

Rousseau, Jean Jacques, 9, 139–142, 145, 147

Rumania, vocational training in, 68

Sagesse et illusions de la philosophie, 56

sciences, teaching of the, 51–55, 90

Scotland, *see* Murray House

secondary education, secondary schools, 11, 14, 48, 55, 57–58, 60, 61, 62, 99, 100, 102, 103, 111, 126; *see also* elementary, primary, programs, training of teachers, *and* vocational

semiotic, *see* symbolic

sensorimotor actions or activities, 29–30, 33, 40

sensorimotor causality, *see* causality

sensorimotor education, 98

sensory education, 34, 97–98

Sergi, Joseph, 147

Sherbrooke (Canada) method, *see* mixed method

Skinner, Burrhus Frederic, 75, 77–78, 79